D0642252

Exploring Our Country

Daniel Wood

General Editors
Carol Langford
Chuck Heath

Teacher Consultant
Vicki Mulligan

Explorations A Canadian Social Studies Program for Elementary Schools

Douglas & McIntyre (Educational) Ltd.
1615 Venables Street
Vancouver, British Columbia V5L 2H1

Canadian Cataloguing in Publication Data

Wood, Daniel.
    Exploring our country

    (Explorations : a Canadian social studies program
for elementary schools. Exploring Canada)
    ISBN 0-88894-863-8

    1. Cities and towns — Canada — Juvenile literature.
2. Community — Juvenile literature.
I. Title. II. Series.
    HT127.W66   j307.7'6   C82-091303-0
Printed and bound in Canada.

A Message from the Author

This book tells you about people and communities in Canada. In writing it, I visited many places. Everywhere I went, people helped out. They told me stories about their lives. I had lunch with a farming family. I watched boats in a canal. I talked about fishing until late one evening. I even played street hockey with some children. Most of all, I remember how friendly everyone was.

Contents

1

How does Morgan discover Canada?

Until she was nine years old, Morgan McCloskey was just like other children. She liked making angels in the snow and eating birthday cakes. She liked collecting bugs and climbing trees. She hated being tickled.

Morgan often explored her town. She was always noticing things. She liked watching workers digging up the streets. She wondered how far the pipes went. She wondered, too, where watermelons came from. She'd never seen any growing in her community. She wondered what happened to all the trees they cut down for lumber near her town. People in her community didn't build *that* many houses.

Morgan wondered about other communities, too. "Are other places like my town?" she would ask herself. She'd never been far from home.

Would you like to visit another community? What would you like to see?

Morgan knew that she lived in British Columbia. But still, she wondered about her own **province**. She'd never even been to Victoria, and Victoria was the **capital** city. And what about the rest of Canada? How could she ever see the whole **country**?

One day something magic happened. Morgan had been sitting in front of the TV. A commercial was on, so she decided to change the channel. Suddenly, the knob came off in her hand.

"Oh no!" she thought. "Now I'll get into trouble."

Morgan tried to push the knob back on. It wouldn't fit. She gave it an enormous shove. The TV began shaking. It started making strange sounds. The picture on the screen turned odd colours. Like magic, the glass in front of the screen slid down. Morgan was amazed.

Morgan put her finger up towards the screen. There was nothing to stop her finger. She could reach right into the picture.

A man in the commercial said, "There's a finger sticking out of the camera."

"Wow!" she thought. "I don't have to *watch* TV anymore. I can be *in* it."

Morgan decided to use her TV to explore Canada. There were lots of things she wanted to find out.

Morgan already knew something about Canada. She knew that it is a big country made up of ten provinces and two **territories**. She also knew there are thousands of different communities all across the land. Some of these communities are huge and some are tiny. There were lots of places Morgan wanted to explore.

She never told anyone about her magic TV set. It was her secret. Not even Morgan's parents knew. "Someday," Morgan told herself, "maybe I'll be a great explorer."

Can you find Victoria, the capital of British Columbia, on the map? The map of Canada also shows the six communities that Morgan will visit. What are the names of those communities?

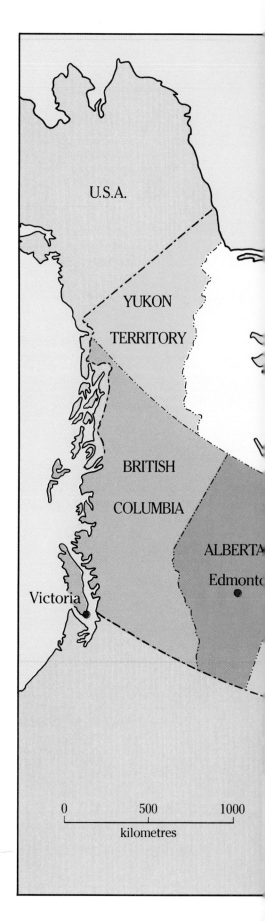

8

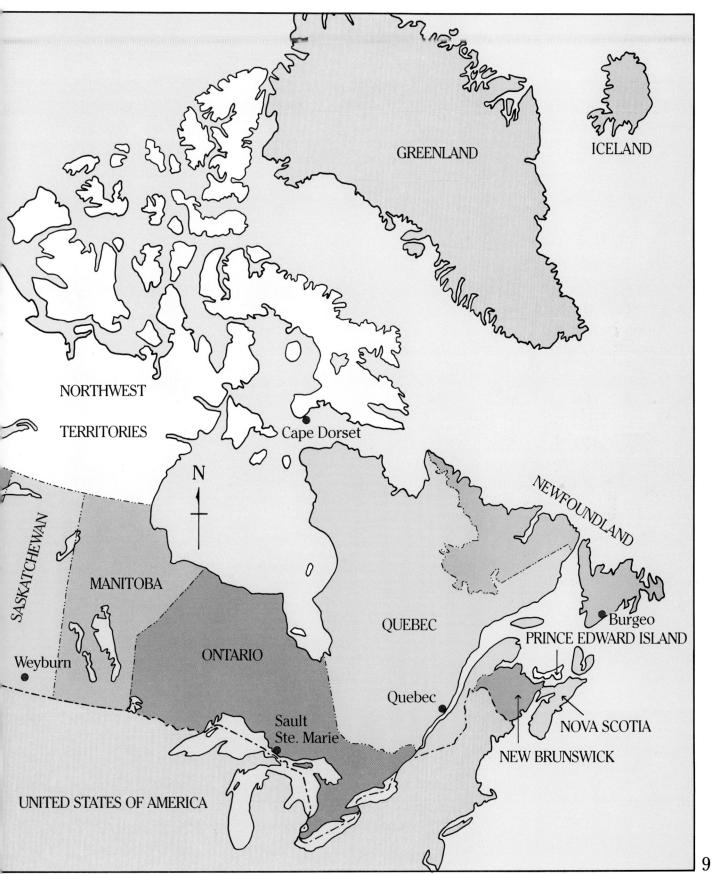

NORTHWEST

TERRITORIES

GREENLAND

ICELAND

Cape Dorset

NEWFOUNDLAND

N

SASKATCHEWAN

MANITOBA

ONTARIO

QUEBEC

Weyburn

Burgeo

PRINCE EDWARD ISLAND

Quebec

Sault
Ste. Marie

NOVA SCOTIA

NEW BRUNSWICK

UNITED STATES OF AMERICA

2

Where does Edmonton's oil go?

It was a rainy Saturday in August. Morgan's parents had gone shopping. Morgan turned on the TV. A reporter was talking about **oil** in Alberta. Oil was making the province rich. The reporter pointed to the machine behind her.

"This **oil well** is an important part of the story of oil. We are a short distance south of Edmonton. Join me for a trip through oil country," the woman said.

"Don't mind if I do," Morgan said to herself. She took a quick look around her living room. Then she climbed into the TV set. Morgan suddenly found herself in a field.

Morgan looked around. She knew Edmonton was a big city, but she couldn't see any buildings. Except for the TV crew, all she could see were fields of wheat. In the fields were strange machines which moved up and down like robots. Morgan wondered where the buildings were.

Page 11: This is one of the oil wells south of Edmonton. The machine pumps oil from deep in the ground. How else is the land used?

Morgan followed the TV crew around. Every once in a while she poked her head into the camera. She wanted to see if her mother and father had come home from shopping. Her living room remained empty. She sat on the ground and watched the TV crew tape the show.

The reporter talked about oil. "This part of Canada was once covered by an ocean. In the time before dinosaurs, plants and small animals lived here. When they died, they fell to the ocean bottom. They were gradually covered up. Millions of years passed. The ocean dried up. Deep in the ground, the dead plants and animals slowly turned into oil."

It took a long, long time for oil to be made. What will we do if we use all our oil?

Working on drilling rigs takes skill and hard work. The drill must go through different layers of rock before it reaches oil.

The woman pointed to a farming **tractor** in the wheat field. "About a hundred years ago, the gasoline engine was invented. Cars and tractors use gasoline made from oil. Soon, a lot of oil was needed for **fuel**. Canada's first oil well was drilled in Ontario. There wasn't very much oil there. People looked for oil in other places."

The reporter then told about the **oil field** around her. "In 1947, oil was found right here. A well was drilled. Oil shot out of the ground. Everyone was very excited. The oil had been trapped underground for millions of years. Now it could be used for fuel."

The woman looked at the machine behind her. "This oil well is called Leduc Number One. It marked the discovery of a very large oil field in Canada. This oil field lies in Leduc, not very far from Edmonton, Alberta."

Tell what happened at Leduc. Why was this important? How do you think Leduc might have changed after the discovery of oil?

February 13, 1947 was the day oil started flowing at Leduc. At first, oil and gas were burned off, making a cloud of smoke. Oil is still pumped from the Leduc oil field.

Edmonton

Getting Oil to People

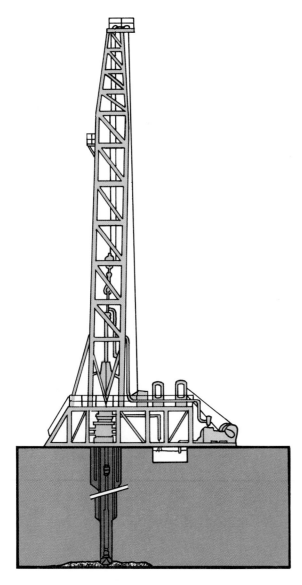

Once the oil is found, ▷ you must get it out of the ground. This special machine pumps out the oil. It's called a "grasshopper." As it moves up and down, it looks like a grasshopper's hind legs. It's also called a "nodding donkey" and a "walking beam." Can you think why?

The oil is sent through a pipeline to an oil **refinery**. There are many oil refineries near Edmonton. An oil refinery isn't just big. It's gigantic. Here oil is made into many different products.

Finding oil is a tricky business. First, you have to drill deep into the earth using a long pipe. Often there is no oil. The well is dry. But if you pick the right spot, oil may come shooting up.

A lot of oil gets shipped through very long pipelines. They take oil all across Canada. Whether you live in Vancouver or Montreal, you might be using oil from Edmonton. The oil may heat your school and run the buses and cars in your community. ▽

Some of the oil becomes fuel for ▷ tractors, cars and airplanes. Some of it becomes grease, asphalt and wax. Some of it is made into hundreds of things you can use.

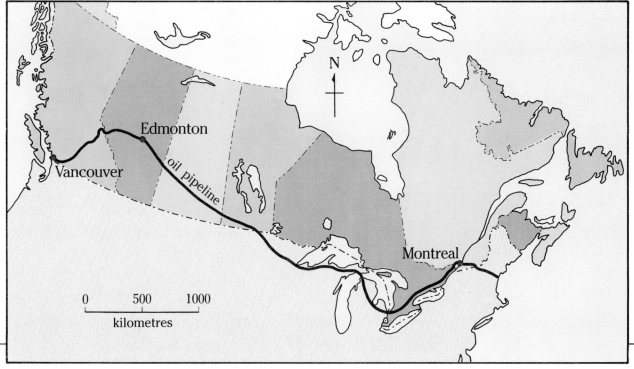

Edmonton

Vancouver

oil pipeline

N

Montreal

0   500   1000

kilometres

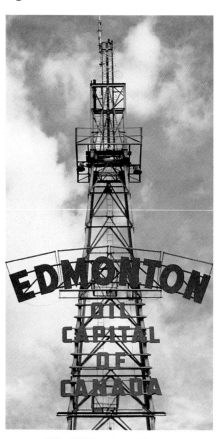

Visitors to Edmonton see this oil rig. What do you think the sign means?

The red light on the front of the camera blinked off. Morgan gasped! She raced up to the camera. She peeked in. There was no living room and no sofa. The camera had been turned off. She was trapped outside her TV set. She was stuck in Edmonton.

Morgan turned to the man with the camera. "Could you turn it on again, just for a second?" She only needed a second to slip back into the camera.

"Sorry, kid," the TV man said. "We're already late." He began to unplug the wires.

Morgan had to think fast. She didn't know anyone in Edmonton. She hadn't thought of bringing her piggy bank. "Hey!" she said. "Need some help? I'll carry those things to the truck."

"No, no. They're too heavy."

"I'm strong," Morgan said. The man let her carry a small case. "I wish I had my own oil well," Morgan said.

The cameraperson laughed. He agreed. "It's the next best thing to having your own money tree."

Morgan thought to herself, "Oil must be worth a lot of money."

Pretend the price of gasoline suddenly doubled. How would your life change?

"Where are you going now?" Morgan asked the cameraperson.

"Next is skunks," he said.

"Skunks?" Morgan repeated. She didn't know much about skunks, but she knew skunks stank.

"We're going to see the skunks of Skunk Hollow," he said. "Skunk Hollow is an old neighbourhood in Edmonton. It's right beside the river and skunks like it there. Some people there like the skunks. Others want to get rid of them. Both groups are holding a parade in half an hour."

Morgan couldn't quite believe her ears. "Can I come?" she asked.

"Sure. Hop in the truck."

Why would some people want to let skunks stay in their neighbourhood? Why would some people want to get rid of the skunks? Are there any animals in your neighbourhood that people don't like?

Many people have come to Edmonton to celebrate the city's past. Compare downtown Edmonton with your community.

The North Saskatchewan River runs through Edmonton. How is the land near the river being used?

The television truck headed north. All around, the land was flat. Soon Morgan could see the office towers in the distance. That was Edmonton. Then they passed **factories** and used car lots and motels along the road. Morgan could see that Edmonton was a big city.

As they got closer into town, Morgan could look over the North Saskatchewan River. The TV truck turned and went down into Skunk Hollow. Morgan got out. A crowd had gathered. Some people carried banners and posters. Someone was dressed up as a giant skunk. One poster read: SAVE OUR SKUNKS. Another one read: NO MORE SKUNKS. There were signs for skunks and signs against skunks.

18

Edmonton

Working for a Better Community

P eople who share the same ideas often get together. They might form a group to improve their community. In every town and city, there are community groups. The people in the group often work as **volunteers**. They do not get paid. They work because they want to help their community. People of all ages can be volunteers.

◁ Some groups work in more than one community. There is a Society for the Prevention of Cruelty to Animals in many places. This group wants everyone to treat animals well.

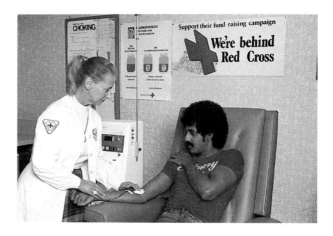

The Red Cross works to save people's lives. There are Red Cross volunteers in large and small communities. These groups link many communities because they are all working for the same goals.

Community groups might write letters to the newspaper. They might write to the **government**. Sometimes they have a parade with posters and banners. Sometimes members of the group talk on radio and TV. The groups want to explain their ideas. They want to get other people involved. When **citizens** work together in a community group, they can get a lot of things done.

SUPPORT BIG SISTERS

21

The crew hurried to set up their cameras. Morgan felt relieved. She knew that now she could get back to her own home, but she wanted to see Skunk Hollow first. People were singing and waving their posters. Someone gave Morgan a poster which read: I LIKE SKUNKS. The person dressed up as the skunk gave out free lollipops, too. Morgan took one.

Morgan looked around Skunk Hollow. There were old houses. Some of the sidewalks were made of wood. She could see the river. There were parks around Skunk Hollow, too.

Morgan listened to people talk about the skunks. Not everyone liked them. Sometimes skunks spray pet dogs and cats. Sometimes they frighten the children. One group wanted to kill the skunks. Other people disagreed. They said that the skunks have a right to live there, too.

The people in Skunk Hollow had a parade. How else could they tell others what they thought about skunks?

What can you learn about Skunk Hollow from the two pictures to the right? Compare Skunk Hollow with your neighbourhood.

22

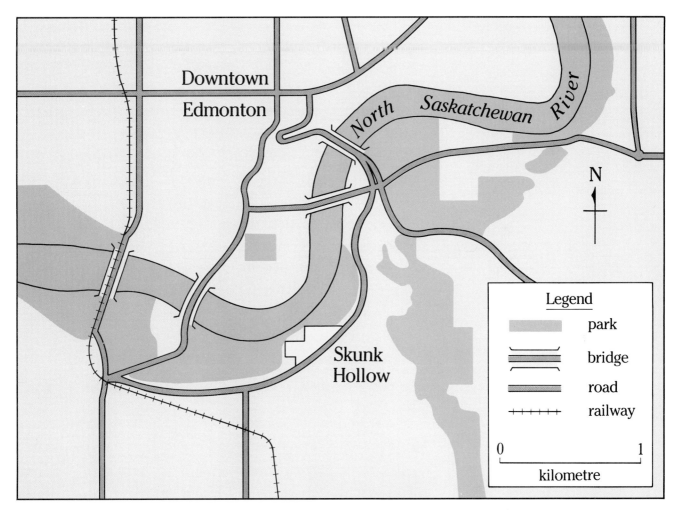

Above: Find Skunk Hollow on the map. Where can cars cross the river? Where can trains cross?

Morgan had almost forgotten about going home. Everyone seemed to be having a good time. The people did not agree about the skunks, but they weren't angry with each other.

Morgan knew it was time to go. She peered into the corner of the TV camera. She could hear her parents talking in the kitchen. Still carrying her lollipop and poster, she climbed into the camera.

Morgan thought to herself, "It was more fun to visit Edmonton than to watch a TV program about it."

When her father came into the living room, he looked surprised. "Ah! There you are," he said, and gave Morgan a kiss.

Morgan took her lollipop out of her mouth. "Dad," said Morgan, "what do you think about skunks?"

"Skunks?" her father replied. "What makes you ask that?"

Morgan shrugged. "Oh, I was just thinking," she said.

Morgan's father shook his head. "Morgan, sometimes you ask the craziest questions."

What did Morgan bring home from Edmonton? What souvenir would you give Morgan if she came to your community?

24

What is your decision?

There are old neighbourhoods on both sides of the river in Edmonton. Skunk Hollow is one of them. Some houses need fixing up, but the people like living there.

There are parks along parts of the river. Some people would like to tear down the old houses to make a park all along the river. Many people live in apartments in downtown Edmonton. They would like more parks.

How do people feel about the old neighbourhoods beside the river?

Why do people in downtown Edmonton need parks?

What will happen to the people whose houses are torn down?

Do you think the old neighbourhoods should be turned into parks?

Thinking about Edmonton

Links with Edmonton

You are learning how communities are linked to one another. Each of these sentences tells one way Edmonton links Canadians. Match each sentence with a picture in this chapter.

1. Canadians use things made with oil from Edmonton.
2. Oil is sent by pipeline from Edmonton to other communities.
3. Volunteer groups do the same kind of work in Edmonton as they do in other communities.

Working Together

Alberta's oil will last longer if we use it wisely. Work with a partner to make a poster. The poster should tell people how to save oil.

Comparing Communities

Make a large chart for comparing communities. Look at the chart below to see the headings. With your class, put information about your community in the top row. Now put information about Edmonton in the second row. Think about ways in which your community is like Edmonton. Think about ways in which it is different.

Community	Products	Transportation	Recreation	Tourist Places	Language
Your Community					
Edmonton					

Reading a Map

This map shows some communities in British Columbia and Alberta. The map has a compass rose. The four main points are north, south, east and west. The points in between are also marked. They are northeast, southeast, southwest and northwest.

Put the edge of your notebook from Edmonton to Calgary. Now look at the compass rose. Find the line from the centre of the compass rose to S (south). This line points in the same direction as the line from Edmonton to Calgary. You would go south to get from Edmonton to Calgary.

1. Put the edge of your notebook from Prince George to Fort Chipewyan. Find the line on the compass rose which points to the northeast. The line from Prince George to Fort Chipewyan points in the same direction. Which direction would you go to get from Prince George to Fort Chipewyan?
2. Pretend that you want to go from Calgary to Fort Nelson. Put your notebook between the two communities. Which direction would you travel?
3. Use the compass rose to find out the direction from Edmonton to Vancouver.

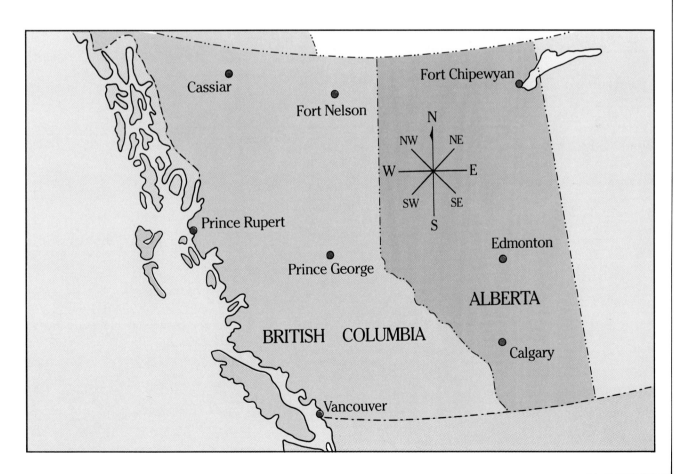

3

How does Weyburn help feed Canadians?

Page 29: This wheat farm is in Saskatchewan. The tractor is pulling a swather. What is the swather doing?

Morgan was crazy about horses. She drew pictures of them with crayons. She collected their photos from magazines. At night she dreamed of them. In her dreams, the horses were always white. The funny thing was, she'd never even ridden a horse.

One afternoon in September, Morgan was sitting alone watching TV. There on the screen was the horse of her dreams. Morgan raced to the hall closet. She grabbed her favourite red scarf. Then she climbed into the TV.

Morgan looked around. Everyone was staring at her. Even the boy on the white horse was staring at her.

"Give that kid something to do before she ruins everything," said a woman with earphones. She didn't look very happy. A pair of hands lifted Morgan up to the cab of a farming tractor.

"Hi," said a friendly man inside the tractor. He was wearing a cap with the word "CO-OP" on it. "You sit beside me here. Do you want to help me drive this tractor?"

Morgan gulped. *Drive* a tractor! She'd never even been inside one before.

Morgan held onto the steering wheel. She was afraid she would crash. She looked around, but there wasn't much to crash into. The tractor was moving across a big, huge, gigantic field. There were no trees and no telephone poles around. The land was absolutely flat.

Why do you think some farmers like flat land? Do all farmers need flat land?

"It's so flat around here! Where are we?" she asked the man beside her.

"This is Saskatchewan," he said. "Weyburn, Saskatchewan, to be exact."

Morgan had never heard of it.

The man in the cap introduced himself. His name was Lars Sondquist. The tractor was on his land. He pointed out the back window. Morgan could see a wide machine that the tractor was pulling. "What's that machine doing?"

"Cutting down the wheat," Mr. Sondquist said. "It's **harvest** time. The TV crew needs pictures of harvesting wheat. They're doing a show about Weyburn."

What does "harvest" mean? What could you harvest besides wheat? If you had a farm, what would you grow?

Mr. Sondquist told Morgan about wheat farming as they rode back and forth across the field. It was a bumpy ride.

A row of machines picks up the wheat after it has been cut. Why do you think a farmer uses so many machines?

Left: A farmer shows part of his wheat crop. What might the wheat be used for?

Weyburn

Growing Wheat on the Prairies

Weyburn, Saskatchewan is found in a part of Canada called the **prairies**. The land there is flat. The **fertile** soil produces good crops. Most farmers on the prairies grow wheat, rye, oats or barley. These are called **grains**.

◁ The farmers near Weyburn mostly grow wheat. The wheat is later made into flour. Then the flour goes into all sorts of things for people to eat.

The farming season begins in the spring after the prairie snow has melted. First, farmers plow the fields to turn the soil. They often plant the seeds at the same time. After the plants have come up, they spray the fields to kill weeds and insects. ▷

By August, the crop is waist high. The wheat is golden yellow. It will soon be time for the harvest. When the weather is perfect, farmers swath, or cut, their fields. All the stalks of grain are cut down and piled in rows to dry. Farmers need dry weather at this time. A few days later, they gather up the wheat. They use a big machine called a **combine**.

The combine separates the kernels of grain from the straw. The grain is loaded into trucks and taken away for storage on the farm. The straw is left lying on the fields.

Morgan sighed. The tractor didn't move very fast. She would rather be riding the white horse.

Finally, they stopped. "Thanks for the help," Mr. Sondquist said. He put his cap on Morgan's head. "Now you're a real farmer."

"You didn't crash," said the boy on the horse, as Morgan jumped down from the tractor.

The boy on the horse was Mr. Sondquist's son. His name was Mark, but everyone called him "Gumbo." In Saskatchewan it can be very muddy at times. It's a sticky, gooey kind of mud called "gumbo." And Gumbo always found ways of getting covered in it. Gumbo introduced his horse. Its name was Stewball. Morgan thought, "They sure have funny names around here." But she still wanted to ride the horse.

Do people ride horses in your community? Would you like to travel by horse?

"You kids meet us back at the farmhouse," Mr. Sondquist said. So Morgan and Gumbo walked towards the yellow building in the distance. Morgan wanted to ride Stewball, but she didn't dare to ask.

A little while later, Mr. Sondquist came home, but the TV crew wasn't with him. "Oh no!" thought Morgan. Without them, she couldn't get back to her own home.

"Where did they go?" Morgan asked.

"To downtown Weyburn," Mr. Sondquist said. "They're going to talk to W.O. Mitchell."

"Who's that?"

"Who's W.O. Mitchell!" Mr. Sondquist said. "He's one of Canada's most famous writers. He used to live in Weyburn. His stories are about life in Weyburn. That's why the TV people are here. They're doing a show about life in Weyburn."

Morgan felt a bit relieved. If she could get to Weyburn, she could find the TV crew again.

Top: Do you think this wheat is ready for harvesting?

Bottom: Combines empty kernels of wheat into trucks. What happens to the straw that is left?

"Do you want to go to Weyburn?" she asked Gumbo.

"Sure. We could take Stewball."

"Good, good, good!" thought Morgan. Instead she said, "I've never ridden a horse in my life."

Gumbo showed Morgan how to climb onto Stewball's back by using the top step of the porch. Together they rode east. "A horse is even bumpier than a tractor," Morgan thought to herself.

It didn't take them very long to reach downtown Weyburn. They crossed a bridge over the Souris River. They went over the train tracks. Beside the tracks stood several tall buildings. Some were painted silver and some were painted red.

Gumbo explained that these were **grain elevators**. They are used for storing grain. That's where Mr. Sondquist would take his wheat. Morgan looked up at the elevator marked "Saskatchewan Pool." It was a **co-operative**. It was owned by the farmers. Gumbo called it a co-op.

Gumbo and Morgan rode Stewball along Third Street. Morgan could see that Weyburn was a small town. It had about 50 stores, and it had only one movie theatre. But it was the biggest town for some distance.

Gumbo explained that most of the people who live in the town work in offices, stores and local factories. Most of the people who live *near* Weyburn are farmers. They come to town to shop or go to a restaurant. It's 135 km (kilometres) from Weyburn to the nearest *big* city. It's called Regina. People go there to watch the football games or for a big shopping trip.

Where does your family go shopping? Do you ever go to a larger community to shop? Why or why not?

Above: The co-op department store is in downtown Weyburn. Who owns a co-op?

Left: Why are the grain elevators beside the railway tracks?

37

Weyburn

Shipping Grain across Canada

After harvesting, farmers take their grain to a grain elevator. There are six grain elevators in Weyburn. Almost every town on the prairies has at least one. The grain is weighed and then lifted to the top of the elevator on a **conveyor**. There it is stored.

During the year, trains come to pick up the grain. They stop at grain elevators all across the prairies. The grain is loaded into **hopper cars**. One hopper car can be loaded in about 20 minutes. Farmers depend on the railways. There is no other way to send their grain across Canada.

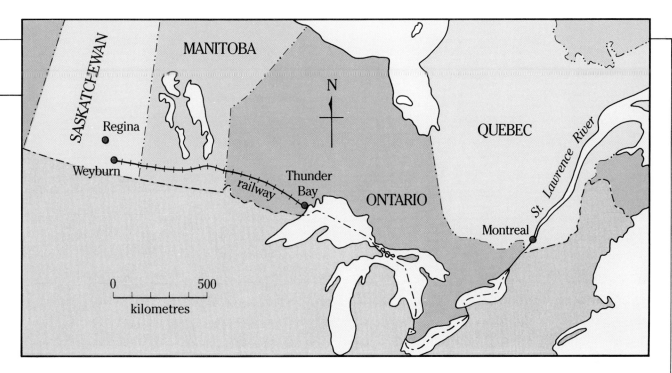

Most of Weyburn's wheat goes by rail to Thunder Bay in Ontario. Thunder Bay is a large grain **port** on the Great Lakes.

At Thunder Bay, the wheat is stored once again, this time in very large **grain terminals**. Huge ships come to get the grain. They take it through the Great Lakes and along the St. Lawrence River.

More than half of Canada's grain is sold to countries around the world. The rest of the wheat stays in Canada. It is taken to flour mills where it is ground up. Shoppers buy flour or bread or cakes all over Canada. These things might have come from the wheat grown near Weyburn.

Top: The prairie crocus is a sign of spring. How do you think farmers might feel when they see the first crocus?

Bottom: W.O. Mitchell has written stories about life on the prairies. Who Has Seen The Wind? *has been made into a movie.*

Morgan liked Weyburn. No one seemed to be in much of a hurry. People stood chatting. Some stopped to talk with Gumbo and Morgan. No one seemed to be racing around.

It was Morgan who was in a hurry. She was afraid of missing the TV truck. "Let's go to W.O. Mitchell's house," Morgan said.

In a few minutes, they'd reached W.O. Mitchell's old home on Sixth Street. Morgan was glad to see the TV crew still there. A small crowd of people had gathered around. A man with white hair sat on the front steps.

The woman with the earphones turned to the crowd. "Any volunteers? We need someone for Mr. Mitchell to tell a story to." She looked at Morgan. "Do you want to be on TV again?"

W.O. Mitchell patted the step beside him. Morgan sat down. The red light on the TV camera blinked on. The camera was taking their picture. Morgan knew she could get back home, so she leaned back against the stairs. Beneath a huge cottonwood tree, she listened to the man beside her tell his story.

It was about life on the prairies when he was a kid. Morgan closed her eyes. She could almost see what Weyburn looked like 60 years before. Mr. Mitchell told about **blizzards** so bad that they covered up whole houses. He told of finding wild crocuses along the banks of the Souris River in the spring. He described summer dust storms that blew the dry soil into the sky. Farmers would lose their crops during those bad years. He also told about the good years when everything went well. The fields of wheat would be golden in September. The farmers would bring in a "bumper crop."

Pretend you are a TV reporter. Write three questions you would ask W.O. Mitchell.

40

Top: What might happen during a dust storm?

Bottom: This snow plow is clearing a highway in Saskatchewan. Why is this work important?

41

Morgan opened her eyes. The man's story was nearing its end. She knew that she had better get back home before the camera blinked off. She waved a tiny goodbye to Gumbo. She waved to Stewball, too. Then she pulled her new cap down tightly on her head. Before anyone realized what was happening, Morgan climbed into the camera.

Morgan's mother had just come home from work. She looked at Morgan and said, "Shouldn't you be doing your school work?"

"I've been learning about horses and wheat," said Morgan. She looked at her mother's face. Morgan knew that her mother didn't really believe her.

What souvenir did Morgan bring back? Why will it remind her of Weyburn?

What is your decision?

Morgan thought about driving the tractor. She liked big machines almost as much as horses. "I'd like to become a farmer," she told Gumbo.

Gumbo was surprised. All the farmers he knew were men. "Farming is hard work," he told Morgan. "Farmers have to drive and fix heavy machines."

Gumbo told Morgan about his mother's work. She looked after the chickens and ran the house. "A farm woman is busy with her own work," Gumbo said. "She wouldn't have time to work in the fields, too."

The farmers that Gumbo knew were men. Does that mean that women cannot become farmers?

Do you think a woman could drive a tractor?

Could a man do the cooking and washing for a farm family?

Do you think that there are men's jobs and women's jobs?

Thinking about Weyburn

Links with Weyburn

In this book you are learning how communities are linked to one another. Each of these sentences tells one way that Weyburn links Canadians. Match each sentence with a picture in this chapter.

1. Grain from Weyburn is used to make food in other communities.
2. A railway takes grain from Weyburn to Thunder Bay.
3. Canadians read W.O. Mitchell's stories about Weyburn.

Working Together

Work with a partner to make a collage. Get some old magazines. Cut out pictures of things made with wheat. Paste the pictures on a large piece of paper. Put the breakfast foods on the left side. Put the lunch foods in the middle. Put the dinner foods on the right side.

Comparing Communities

Add Weyburn to your Comparing Communities chart. Put information about Weyburn in its row. Now compare your community with Weyburn. How are they the same? How are they different?

Community	Products	Trans-portation	Recreation	Tourist Places	Language
Your Community					
Weyburn					

This is a map of Weyburn. Find the scale line at the bottom of the map. You can use the scale line to measure distances on the map.

This is how to use the scale line. Take a strip of paper about 15 cm (centimetres) long. Hold it next to the scale line. Draw tiny lines on the paper to match the lines on the scale line. Print numbers on your strip of paper. These tell you the distance on the ground in metres. Print 100 under the first tiny line, 200 under the second one, and so on. Now your strip of paper looks like a ruler. It can be used to measure the map. Then you will know the distance on the ground, too.

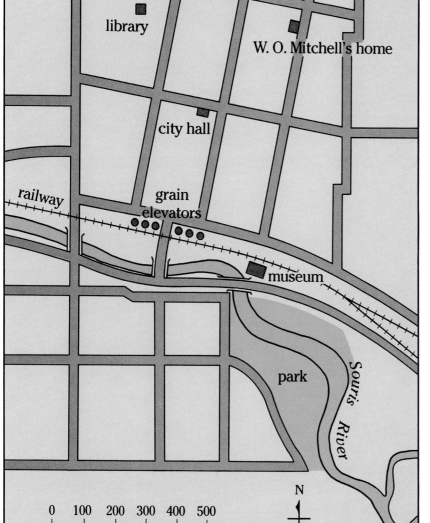

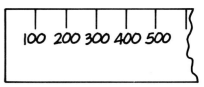

1. Use your strip of paper to measure the distance from the school to city hall. How many metres is it?
2. Use your strip of paper to measure the distance from W.O. Mitchell's home to the museum. How long do you think it would take you to walk that far?
3. Pick two places on the map. Use your strip of paper to measure the distance between them.

4

Why is Sault Ste. Marie a Canadian crossroad?

Page 47: In the front of the picture you can see the American canals. In the back of the picture you can see the Canadian canal at Sault Ste. Marie. How is this picture like a map?

Morgan sat up and listened. "The top news story is from Sault Ste. Marie, Ontario," said the woman on the TV. "A grain ship on Lake Superior is in danger of sinking. Here's our reporter at the scene."

On the screen appeared a man all bundled up. Snow swirled about his face. "The laker, *North Wind II*, has been caught in this winter's first storm. The ship may have already gone down. We're standing beside the Sault Ste. Marie **Canal**. Family and friends of the ship's crew are waiting here for news."

Morgan dashed to her room. She pulled on her long underwear. Then she pulled on her ski suit and wool hat. She wrapped her favourite red scarf around her neck as she ran downstairs.

It was a tight squeeze climbing into the TV set. She almost got stuck.

"What's happening?" Morgan asked a man with snow in his beard.

"A ship's lost in the blizzard," he told her. "I wouldn't want to be out on Lake Superior on a night like this. It has killed a lot of good sailors over the years. Well, no use for us to freeze out here. Do you want a cup of tea? Sassafras, mint, orange pekoe? You name it and I've got it."

Imagine what it would be like to be out in a blizzard. What would you see? What would you hear? What would you feel?

"Sassafras tea!" Morgan thought. She had never heard such a silly name. But the idea of something warm sounded good. She followed the man into a small building right beside the canal. Three other men sat inside. They were playing cards. A man on TV was talking about the Grey Cup football game. He mentioned the Edmonton Eskimos. It reminded Morgan of her trip to Edmonton. The man with the beard put a kettle on the stove.

Top: A road bridge and a railway bridge cross the St. Mary's River. They join Canada and the United States. What is the river like between the bridges?

Bottom: The lock master stands beside the Canadian lock.

"Sit yourself down," he said, pointing to a couch. Morgan sat herself down. "I'm Erik Tikkanen. I'm the lock master," he said. "These are my helpers. When a ship comes, we open the **lock** on the Sault Ste. Marie Canal."

"Are you waiting for the ship that's lost?" Morgan asked.

"You bet," said Erik. He poured the tea. It did taste good.

Erik was listening for the ship's whistle. He gave Morgan a card showing the whistle **signals**. All ships use the same signals. While they waited for the ship, Erik explained to Morgan how a lock works.

Why do ships use whistle signals? What kinds of signals do you use?

Sault Ste. Marie

Moving Ships through the Locks

St. Mary's River is between two large lakes. One lake is Lake Superior and the other is Lake Huron. There are **rapids** in the river. Long ago, canoes could go through part of the rapids. But they couldn't go through the rockiest part. People had to carry their canoes along the river bank.

Canals and locks were built at Sault Ste. Marie so that ships could get past the rapids. A canal is a waterway which people have made. Locks in canals are used to raise or lower ships. Then they can go from one lake to another.

upper gate

lower gate

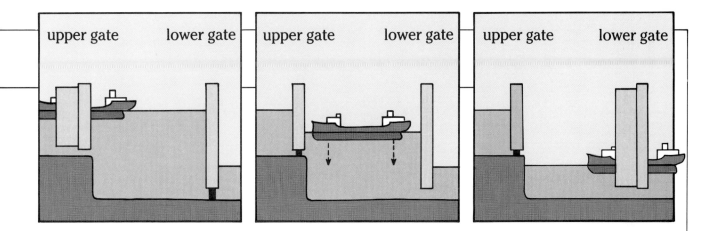

Lake Superior is 6 m (metres) higher than Lake Huron. Ships can be taken up or down in a lock. A ship from Lake Superior enters a lock which is full of water. The water is the same height as Lake Superior. Then the lock master pushes two buttons. The water beneath the ship drains out. It's like pulling the plug in a bathtub. The lock takes about 15 minutes to drain. Slowly the ship is lowered. It goes down to the height of Lake Huron. When the water is low enough, the gates in front of the ship open. The ship sails out of the lock towards Lake Huron. What happens when a ship goes the other way, from Lake Huron to Lake Superior?

The border between Canada and the United States goes through the St. Mary's River. Today there is one lock on the Canadian side of the river. It is the oldest lock. Many small pleasure boats use the Canadian lock. There are four larger locks on the American side of the river. They are used by most big ships. Ten thousand ships pass through the locks every year.

Suddenly a voice came over the two-way radio in the canal office. Everyone looked up. "VDX-23. VDX-23. This is *North Wind II* calling the Soo. Can you hear me?"

One of the men threw down his cards. He raced to the two-way radio. "This is VDX-23," he answered. "Come in *North Wind II*."

"This is Captain Carlson. It's good to hear you. We'd lost our power for a while. It looked like we might not make it."

"Are you okay now?"

"Yep," said the captain of the missing ship. "It's a bit stormy out here still. But we'll make it." The men in the canal office cheered.

An hour later, Morgan heard a ship's whistle. She looked at her card of whistle signals.

Visitors can watch boats in the Canadian lock. The lower gate is open. What has happened to the boat?

"There she is," Erik shouted.

They all pulled on their coats and dashed outdoors. Morgan could see the ship's bow appear through the blowing snow. She could see the name *North Wind II* up high near the deck. The ship was covered in ice.

The people waiting beside the canal cheered as the ship came in. The TV camera took everyone's picture. The *North Wind II* had made it through Lake Superior. It had reached Sault Ste. Marie safely.

Think about the people beside the canal. List three words which tell how they felt *before* the ship came in. Then list three words which tell how they felt *after* the ship got in.

Top: What can you tell about Sault Ste. Marie from this picture?

Bottom: Describe this street in downtown Sault Ste. Marie.

Sault Ste. Marie

Linking Communities along the Great Lakes

There are five lakes that make up the Great Lakes. There are rivers joining the lakes to one another. Lake Superior is the largest lake. In fact, Lake Superior is the second largest lake in the world. Old sailors say that the lake has two temperatures. They say that one temperature is solid ice and the other is melted ice. It is a very cold lake!

Thousands of ships have sunk in the Great Lakes. The worst time is late November, just before the lakes freeze around the shore. A ship may get caught in a winter storm. It may get covered with ice and sometimes it sinks like a stone. Because of the ice, no ships can sail in the winter.

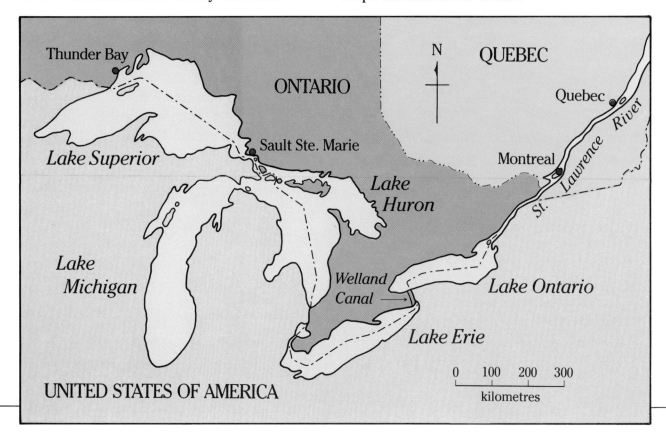

Thunder Bay is the main Canadian port △ at the western end of the Great Lakes. Grain from the prairies is loaded onto ships here. Ships going to or from Thunder Bay pass through the locks at Sault Ste. Marie.

Ships going from Lake Erie to Lake Ontario pass through the Welland Canal. They must go through eight locks. It takes 13 hours for a ship to go through all these locks. The locks are like elevators, taking ships up or down. After leaving Lake Ontario, ships can sail along the St. Lawrence River. They go through several more locks before reaching Montreal or Quebec City. Some ships even go across the ocean to Europe. ◁

What might this skier be carrying for his cross-country ski trip?

It was the first snowstorm of the winter in Sault Ste. Marie. Everyone wanted to go cross-country skiing. Captain Carlson and the crew had to stay with their ship. Erik and Morgan and some of the TV crew piled into Erik's truck.

"Where are we going?" Morgan asked.

"Up to Hiawatha Lodge," Erik said. "We've got a cross-country ski club up there. There are trails through the trees."

Morgan was glad she'd brought her warmest clothes. She liked skiing. She did it a lot back home.

When they arrived at the ski lodge, a party was going on. Many of the people spoke a language Morgan couldn't understand. Even Erik was speaking it. Suddenly, Morgan felt a bit like a stranger. She felt shy. Several children her age were standing by a huge table covered with food. They were helping themselves, eating.

"Hmmmmm," Morgan thought. "FOOD!" Morgan knew she didn't know much about **foreign** languages. She did know a lot about food. Her shyness changed quickly to hunger. When she joined the other children, even the food looked strange to Morgan.

Do you speak another language? Would you like to learn other languages? Why or why not?

"What's this?" Morgan said to a girl with braids. It looked like stew.

"My mom calls it **lanttu laatikko**," she answered.

"What's in it?" Morgan asked. She'd never heard of *lanttu laatikko*.

"It's a turnip casserole."

Morgan didn't particularly like the sound of it. She pointed at the other dishes. She asked the girl with braids what they were.

"This soup here," said the girl, pointing, "is called *mojakka*. And these buns stuffed with potatoes are called *piirakka*. And this coffee cake is called *pulla*."

Morgan felt starved. She took a bite of the coffee cake.

"Why is everyone talking a different language and eating strange food?" Morgan asked.

"Oh! Don't you know?" the girl said. "This is a Finnish club. Most of the people here were born in Finland or have **ancestors** from there. Many Finnish people live around Sault Ste. Marie. My mom says it looks just like Finland here."

If you could move to another country, what things would you like to stay the same? What things would you like to be different?

The Soo Finnish Club runs Hiawatha Lodge. It is a good place to relax after skiing.

57

Morgan didn't feel so shy anymore. She understood why things were different now. She'd never heard anyone speaking Finnish before. She'd never eaten Finnish food. She introduced herself to the other children. And they introduced themselves to her. The girl with the braids was named Alice.

Alice explained that everyone had come to the lodge to practise skiing. They were getting ready for the winter *loppet*.

"What's a *loppet*?" Morgan asked. She had never heard that word before either.

"It means fun race," Alice said. She told Morgan that in many countries of northern Europe, whole communities get together to ski. Old and young people all ski together. They ski through the woods along a set course. It doesn't matter who finishes the route first. It doesn't matter who wins. It's all just for fun.

Alice explained that there was a really big *loppet* in March around Hiawatha Lodge. Hundreds and hundreds of people came. They came from Quebec, Ontario, Manitoba and Saskatchewan. They would all race through the woods on skis. It was a good way to meet old friends and to make new friends.

Page 59, top: Some skiers arrive by train. Do you think this is a good way to travel?

Page 59, bottom: Why is cross-country skiing a good sport?

Morgan borrowed some skis and joined the people practising for the *loppet*. She loved skiing. Alice taught her some Finnish words as they glided across the new snow. When they returned, Morgan saw that the TV crew had set up their camera. Morgan decided she'd better not lose her chance. She poked her head in front of the camera.

"**Hyvästi**," she said in her best Finnish. Then she slipped into the camera. Instantly she was back in her own home.

Morgan's father came into the living room. "Was that you I heard just now speaking some foreign language?"

Morgan smiled. "Yep. *Hyvästi* is the Finnish way of saying goodbye."

Morgan's father looked at his daughter suspiciously. "Since when do you speak foreign languages?" he said.

"Since today," Morgan answered. Then, she went upstairs to change.

Morgan speaks English, so Finnish is a foreign language to her. Where is *English* a foreign language?

60

What is your decision?

Sault Ste. Marie is a **multi-cultural** community. This means that people there have different **cultural** backgrounds. They may talk different languages, eat different foods, and wear different clothes. **Culture** includes the way people think and live, too.

Alice's parents came from Finland. Alice speaks Finnish as well as English. Her family likes Finnish food.

Sometimes people make jokes about people from other cultures. They say mean things about the way they talk, the food they eat or the way they look. These jokes hurt people's feelings. Alice doesn't like hearing them, so she talked to her family.

"Just ignore the jokes," her mother said. "Then the problem will go away."

Alice's father told her, "People make fun of other people just to make *themselves* feel better."

"People *are* different," said Alice's brother. "So it's all right to tell those jokes."

Why do you think some people tell jokes about other people?

How would you feel if someone told a joke about you?

What is the best thing to do when you hear jokes about other people?

Thinking about Sault Ste. Marie

Links with Sault Ste. Marie

In this book you are learning how communities are linked to one another. Each of these sentences tells one way that Sault Ste. Marie links Canadians. Match each sentence with a picture in this chapter.

1. The locks let ships travel from Lake Superior to Lake Huron.
2. Visitors to Sault Ste. Marie come by railway.
3. People from other communities visit Sault Ste. Marie for cross-country skiing.

Working Together

Learn about a different culture from someone in your community. Work in small groups. Decide which culture you would like to learn about. Then make a plan to invite someone from your community to teach you about that culture.

Comparing Communities

Add Sault Ste. Marie to your Comparing Communities chart. Put information about Sault Ste. Marie in its row. In which column is Sault Ste. Marie least like other communities on your chart?

Community	Products	Transportation	Recreation	Tourist Places	Language
Your Community					
Sault Ste. Marie					

Reading a Graph

This graph tells how much snow falls in Sault Ste. Marie each month. The letters at the bottom of the graph stand for the months of the year. The first J stands for January. Can you name the months the other letters stand for?

The bars tell us how much snow usually falls each month in Sault Ste. Marie. The taller the bar, the more snow falls that month.

1. Which are the two snowiest months in Sault Ste. Marie? How much snow usually falls in each of those months? Use a metre stick to see how deep the snow would be.
2. Which months do not usually get any snow?
3. Using the bars, find out how much snow usually falls each month. How much snow usually falls in a whole *year* at Sault Ste. Marie? Think of some games children in Sault Ste. Marie might play at recess during the winter months.

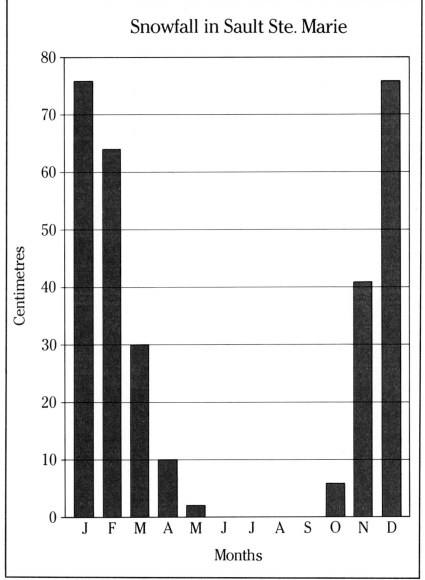

Snowfall in Sault Ste. Marie

5

Why do people like to visit Quebec City?

How is street hockey different from ice hockey?

Morgan jumped down from the TV camera. She couldn't believe her eyes. Right in front of her was the ugliest and angriest face she had ever seen.

"Maybe I've travelled down the wrong channel," Morgan thought. She had wanted to see Canada's biggest winter event. It is held each February in Quebec City. The event is called *Le Carnaval de Québec*. People come from all over Canada and the United States to the ten-day festival.

Morgan listened to the voices around her. It didn't sound like a carnival. In fact, everyone was shouting in French. The boy with the ugly goalie mask was shouting loudest of all.

"This is our street!" he announced as he waved his hockey stick.

A man leaned out of the window of his car. "Streets are for cars, not for hockey games."

"We're practising for the championship in street hockey. We need the street to get ready," said a young girl.

The man in the car began beeping his horn. Other cars behind him joined in.

The boy with the ugly mask sat down on the curb. He pushed up the mask. His friends joined him on the curb. They all looked sad. Morgan sat down with them.

"It's not very fair," said Morgan.

The children agreed. "Do you speak French?" one of them asked.

"A little bit. I'm learning it in school," Morgan said.

"Good!" the others said. They all spoke French. Their names were Maria, Brian, Pierre, Daniel, Michelle and Renée.

Why do the children speak French? Imagine that you are visiting Quebec City. What would you do if you couldn't speak French?

Morgan saw a pair of huge, white feet in front of her. She looked up. It looked like a gigantic snowman, but she knew it was a man dressed up as a snowman.

Bonhomme is standing in front of a snow sculpture. Why is Bonhomme a good symbol for Carnival?

Page 67, top: Different groups try to build the best snow sculpture. What sculpture would you like to make for Carnival?

Page 67, bottom: People from Calgary are making pancakes. What symbol shows that they come from western Canada?

"Bonhomme! Bonhomme!" the children cried. "The King of Carnival."

"No one should be sad during Carnival," Bonhomme said. "What's the matter?"

The children explained their problem and Bonhomme listened. Finally he invited them to join him in his horse-drawn carriage. He told them he had some friends who might know what to do.

The carriage went down a street called *rue Ste-Thérèse*. It was jammed with people. Lights had been strung across the street. People sold souvenirs and clothes and food. Some of the people selling food wore cowboy hats. They were making pancakes right there on the sidewalk. Bonhomme told Morgan that those people were from Calgary, Alberta. They had come across Canada to help the people in Quebec City celebrate.

Does your community have any festivals? How do people celebrate? Do people visit from other places?

Many of the houses along *rue Ste-Thérèse* had big snow sculptures in front of them. Some of these looked like Bonhomme. Others looked like dragons and even baseball players. Everyone in the street waved or tooted on long, red plastic trumpets as Bonhomme passed. Morgan and the street hockey players and Bonhomme waved back.

Snow sculptures on rue Ste-Thérèse *are an exciting part of Carnival. What other special things could you do at a winter festival?*

Morgan loved riding inside the horse-drawn carriage. It was cold outside, but she felt warm. Everyone had snuggled under a big warm rug. Bonhomme pointed out the sights. To Morgan's eyes, Quebec City looked very, very old. She had never seen buildings and streets like this anywhere else. They looked older than the ones in Edmonton or Weyburn or Sault Ste. Marie.

Why do you think the buildings in Quebec City are so old? How old are buildings in your community?

Just then, Morgan saw a white castle. It looked like a castle from a fairy tale, but it was made entirely of snow. It was much bigger than a house, and people could go inside. Bonhomme explained that the castle was part of Carnival. Morgan wanted to stop, but Bonhomme told the driver to go on. Bonhomme was taking the children to a building just behind the snow castle. It is called the National Assembly Building.

Below: During Carnival, there is a boat race across the river. What do you think happens when there is ice in the river?

Above: Tourists can travel around the city by horse and carriage.

Quebec City

Visiting a Historic City

When people visit Quebec City, they like to learn about its history. The city is very old. A French explorer built a trading post here almost 400 years ago. French explorers travelled with Indian guides far into Canada. They started new trading posts.

Early settlers to Quebec City started farms, churches and schools. Some of the oldest buildings in Canada are here. In **Place Royale** some of the buildings are over 300 years old.

Part of Quebec City is high above the St. Lawrence River. Walls were built around the city and there was a fort at the highest point. The army could see if enemy ships were coming.

The early French settlers made many beautiful things with their hands. They did weaving, carving and painting. Visitors can see early art in museums and churches. Quebec artists still make beautiful crafts. ▽

People who visit another community for pleasure are called **tourists**. Many come for Winter Carnival or to see the old city. They might stay in this hotel, built around 1890. Tourists buy meals and souvenirs, and take trips. Many people in Quebec City have jobs taking care of tourists.

Quebec City is the capital of the province of Quebec. People all over the province **elect** men and women to form the government. The elected group is called the National Assembly. It meets in Quebec City to make **laws** for the province of Quebec. When people want help from the government, they can write or phone or go to the National Assembly Building. It has many offices inside.

Where does your provincial government meet to make laws?

Morgan and the street hockey players followed Bonhomme into the building. Signs told Morgan about the different jobs that the government does. Bonhomme led them to the far end of the hall. He was taking them to see the **premier**.

"Wow!" Morgan thought to herself. "The premier! Bonhomme is going to talk to the head of the entire government of Quebec."

"Mr. Premier," said Bonhomme, "my friends have a problem. They're feeling sad. No one should feel sad during Carnival."

"What's the problem?" the premier asked the children.

"We've lost our place where we play street hockey," said Daniel, the boy with the goalie mask.

"So how can we practise for the championship?" Maria asked.

Morgan wanted to say something, too. She felt a little shy. She gulped and said, "They *are* very good. I've seen them on TV. That's why I came to Quebec City."

"Well," the premier said, touching Morgan on the shoulder. "Our visitor here wants you to play street hockey. Bonhomme doesn't want you to be sad. I want you to play your best. So, I'll see what I can do."

The children thanked the premier and left to wait outside his office. Bonhomme had to get back to Carnival. Before he left, he gave the children a souvenir. It was a tiny statue of himself. Then he wished them good luck.

The premier of Quebec made several phone calls. Every time the message was the same. "Do you have a safe place for some children to practise hockey?"

"Sure," said the priest at a small church on *rue Ste-Thérèse*. "They can practise in the parking lot beside the church."

This is the National Assembly Building in Quebec City. What happens here?

Quebec City

Making Government Work for You

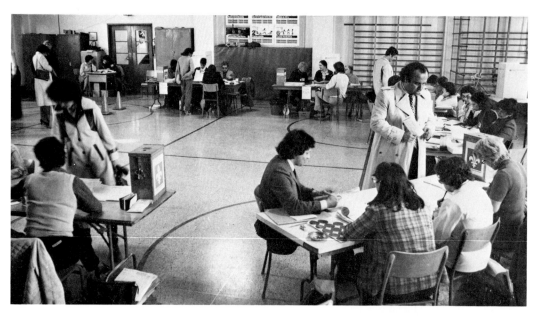

Quebec City is the capital of the province of Quebec. This means the government for the whole province of Quebec meets here. All across Quebec, women and men are chosen in **elections**. People in every community vote for the person they want. The person who is elected represents that community in the government.

The elected people meet in the National Assembly Building in Quebec City. They tell the government what their communities want. Of course, not all communities want the same things. The elected men and women debate and argue. They decide what laws are best for all.

74

Sometimes the people of the province do not like what the government decides. They might hold a parade to show their ideas. Then at the next election the people might vote for someone else. They can choose a new government. In that way the people can make the government work for them.

In Quebec, most people speak French. They want to keep their language and culture. The government gives money for festivals which celebrate Quebec's culture. It has also passed laws about the French language. French is the everyday language of work and government.

Right: Tourists to Carnival like to visit the snow castle. How do you think the castle is made?

Below: Most people in Quebec speak French. What do you think the sign means?

When the premier joined the children again, he was smiling. "We've found a new place for you to practise." He told them about the church parking lot.

"Hooray!" the street hockey players shouted. They all raised their sticks in the air as if they had just scored a goal.

"Hooray!" Morgan shouted, too.

Just before they left, the premier gave Morgan a blue and white flag of Quebec as a souvenir of her visit. Her new friends had to hurry back home. They had to practise for the championship. Morgan wanted to see the snow castle.

"**Au revoir**," they all said to Morgan. Morgan said goodbye to them, too.

Morgan started to race downhill towards the snow castle. In the day's last sunlight, it looked like it was made of vanilla ice cream. Just then a TV truck pulled up. The crew began setting up the cameras. From the door of the National Assembly Building, the premier of Quebec appeared. He was going to make a speech.

Who is the premier of your province? Who represents your community in your provincial government?

Morgan knew that this was her chance to get back home. It was getting late. She'd have to see the snow castle on her next visit. Morgan got near the camera. Then she made her move. "*Au revoir*, Quebec City," she said as she disappeared.

A few days later, she saw Daniel and Maria on TV. The team had come in third in the street hockey championship.

"Hooray!" Morgan shouted and danced around the house.

"You act like you practically know them," Morgan's mother said.

"I do," Morgan replied.

"Don't be silly," Morgan's mother said. "You've never even been to Quebec City."

What is your decision?

Many tourists visit Quebec City. They come from all over Canada. Many of them do not speak French. They speak English in restaurants and hotels and on buses.

Most of the people living in Quebec City speak French. It is the first language they spoke at home. We call this their **mother tongue**. Many of them have learned English, too. When tourists come, they often switch languages and speak English. The children playing street hockey spoke French together. They knew English, too. They could speak English with Morgan.

Could people in your community speak French if French-speaking tourists visited?

How do you think the people of Quebec feel when they must speak English?

How do you think tourists to Quebec City feel if they cannot speak French?

Would it be a good idea for Canadians to learn both French and English?

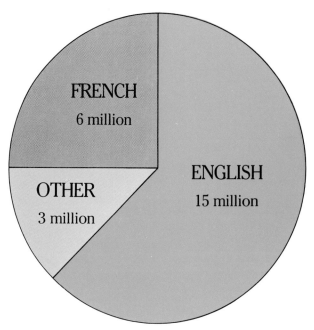

Mother Tongues in Canada (1981)

Street signs in Montreal.

Thinking about Quebec City

Links with Quebec City

In this book you are learning how communities are linked to one another. Each of these sentences tells one way that Quebec City links Canadians. Match each sentence with a picture in this chapter.

1. People visit Quebec City for Winter Carnival.
2. Tourists visit Quebec City to learn about Canada's past.
3. People from each community in Quebec are elected to make laws for everyone in the province.

Working Together

Work in small groups. Half the groups can make a list of reasons people like to visit Quebec City. Then they can make a brochure with pictures telling tourists about Quebec City. The other groups can make a brochure about your own community. Compare the brochures.

Comparing Communities

Add Quebec City to your Comparing Communities chart. Put information about Quebec City in its row. In which column is Quebec City most like other communities on your chart?

Community	Products	Trans-portation	Recreation	Tourist Places	Language
Your Community					
Quebec City					

Reading a Map

This is a map of Quebec City. Look at the numbers along the sides of the map. Look at the letters across the top and bottom of the map. These numbers and letters can help you find places on the map. The lines divide the map into squares. It is called a grid.

Start in the top left corner of the map. The square in the top left corner is 1A. It is in row 1 and column A.

1. Find square 2C. It is in row 2 and column C. What building is in square 2C?
2. Visitors to Quebec City like to stay in a building in square 3C. What is that building?
3. Find the National Assembly Building. What square is it in?
4. Some of Canada's oldest buildings are in *Place Royale*. This area is in two squares on the map. Describe the location of *Place Royale* using the numbers and letters. Remember to describe the row first and the column second. Do this for both squares.

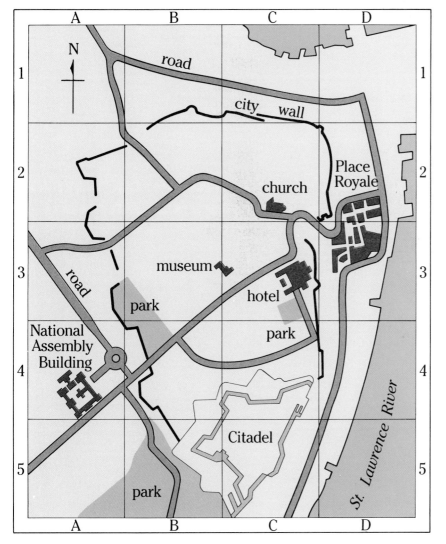

81

6

Will the new road help the people of Burgeo?

One of the TV crew looked up. "Oh no! It's the girl with the red scarf again. She's always interrupting things."

Morgan hadn't meant to interrupt, but it's not every day you get invited to a birthday party. Actually, Morgan hadn't been invited. She had—in her usual way—simply dropped in. The birthday cake looked awfully good. It had 113 candles on it.

The TV announcer had said that Mrs. Gertrude Parker was Canada's oldest citizen. And today, March 4th, was her birthday. So the camera crew had come to Burgeo, Newfoundland where she lived. They were going to put her birthday party on TV. Morgan didn't know anything about Burgeo. She'd never heard of it. She did know something about birthday cakes. She liked them a lot.

"Many of Mrs. Parker's relatives still live here in Burgeo," the announcer had said. "Practically all of them have shown up for the party."

Make a chart of all your relatives. List where they live. How many live in your community? Where do the others live?

The place was indeed packed. There were old people and young people and people in between. A girl Morgan's age introduced herself. Her name was Cammy. She said that Mrs. Parker was her great-great-great-grandmother. Morgan had never heard of a great-great-great-grandmother before.

Burgeo is on the coast of Newfoundland. What are some good things about living beside the ocean?

What can you tell about Burgeo from these photographs?

"She's 112 years old," Cammy told her.

Someone started lighting the candles on the cake. Morgan had never seen so many candles on one cake. Everybody gathered around.

"I can't blow out 112 candles all by myself," said Mrs. Parker. "Somebody's got to help me."

"113!" Cammy shouted. "There's one to grow on."

The lights were turned off. Someone started singing *Happy Birthday*. Soon everyone was singing. Then everybody leaned toward the cake and blew. Morgan helped out. "Ffffffffffffft!" In a second, the candles had all been blown out. Everybody cheered. Mrs. Parker cut the cake. Morgan made sure she got a piece.

The TV reporter interviewed Mrs. Parker. She told him how life had changed in Burgeo during the last hundred years.

Would you like to live in one town all your life? Why or why not?

84

Burgeo

Living in Changing Times

Burgeo is a small fishing town of 2800 people. It is an **outport** on the south coast of Newfoundland. When Mrs. Parker was a girl, the town was very isolated. It was not easy to get to Burgeo. There was no road to Burgeo. Few people ever visited the town or left it. The people often built their own homes, boats and furniture. They made their own clothes. The people liked living there. Everyone knew everyone else. Everyone helped everyone else out.

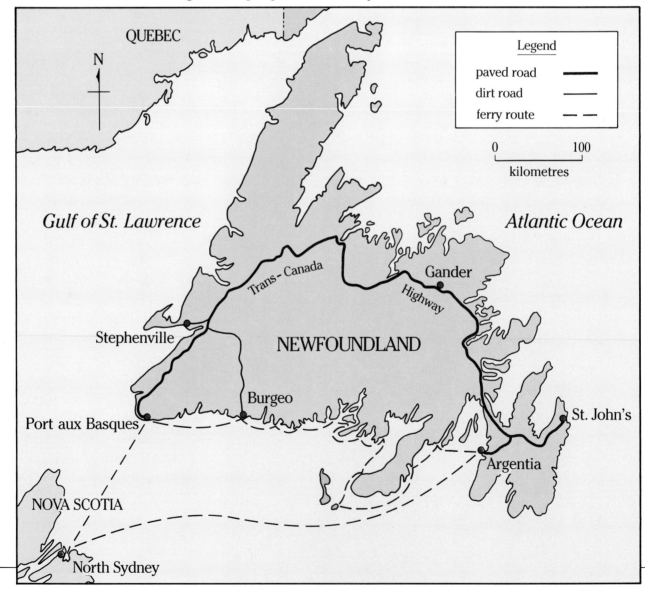

△ There is a ferry that stops at outports along the coast. Travel by boat is still important, but Burgeo has changed. It is not as isolated as it once was. In the 1960s the town got electricity, running water and sewers. The town also began to get TV programs.

In 1979, a road was finally built. The road goes north from Burgeo to the nearest big town called Stephenville. The road crosses 200 km of wilderness. Now, people from Burgeo go shopping in Stephenville. They can buy their furniture, clothes and food there. Although it's only a dirt road, most people are glad to have it. They say it has made Burgeo a better place to live. Mrs. Parker disagrees. She liked Burgeo when it was more isolated. She says that Burgeo was a friendlier place then. She says that people watch too much TV now and don't come visiting often enough.

Through the window of Mrs. Parker's house, Morgan could see the **ocean**. It seemed to be full of **islands**. Waves were crashing against the rocks along the **shore**. Nearby, a red fishing boat had begun pulling up to a **wharf**. Morgan could hear the boat's tooting. She could see the seagulls circling overhead.

Are boats important in your community?

Morgan said to Cammy, "Hey! Here come some more people."

Cammy looked. "That's my dad," she said. She dashed for the door.

"Can I come?" Morgan called.

"Sure. Come on!" Cammy said.

Morgan would have liked another piece of cake, but she didn't want to appear greedy. So she raced

Above: How might the children feel about riding in their cart?

Right: You can see some of the islands near Burgeo. How would you describe an island?

88

after Cammy, Morgan could see lots of fishing boats.

"You've almost missed the party," Cammy called to her father.

"Oh no!" he shouted over the boat's engine. He jumped up onto the dock.

"We already sang *Happy Birthday,*" Cammy said.

"But there's still some cake," Morgan added.

Cammy's father rushed uphill to the party. Cammy and Morgan remained beside the boat. The other fisherman on the boat was named Cecil. He was tying the boat to the wharf with thick ropes.

"Did you catch any fish?" Morgan asked Cecil.

"Oh, one or two," Cecil said, winking at Cammy.

"Is that all?" Morgan asked. She had never caught a fish herself, but then she didn't fish for a living. It was Cecil's job to catch fish and one or two didn't seem like very many fish.

Left: What is this family doing? **89**

Morgan asked if she could see the boat. Cecil helped Cammy and Morgan onto the deck.

"Whoa!" Morgan thought as the deck rocked beneath her feet. She could barely stand. The ocean waves made the boat bounce around. To Morgan it felt like she was on a trampoline.

"Haven't you got your sea legs yet?" Cecil asked with a smile.

"I've got mine," Cammy said. She had often gone out fishing with her father.

Morgan was a "landlubber." This is what sailors call people who usually stay on the land. Cecil and Cammy showed Morgan around the deck of the fishing boat. It was called a **longliner**. Morgan learned that the front of a boat is called the bow and the back is called the stern. The right-hand side of a boat is called the starboard and the left-hand side is called the port.

The boat had a big drum in the back called a gurdy. This machine helps pull in the fish lines. Morgan saw the lines all piled up in a big tub. They were full of seaweed, but contained no fish. In the cabin, Cecil showed her the radar, which helps the crew find their way during foggy weather. He showed her the depth sounder, which helps them find the schools of fish. Morgan even tried the wheel.

Not all boats have a depth sounder. How else would the crew know where to fish?

What things can you see on this longliner? What do you think they are used for?

Burgeo

Fishing off the Coast of Newfoundland

In Burgeo, there are two main types of fishing boats. The most common are the longliners. These boats are about 15 m long. They only go 20 or 30 km away from Burgeo to fish.

The longliners use a fishing line that may be over 1 km long. Hanging down from this long rope are up to 500 shorter fishing lines. Each of these has a baited hook. The crew spend a day out fishing, then come back to Burgeo every evening.

The other main type of fishing boat in △ Burgeo is called a **trawler**. It is three times as big as a longliner. It often has a crew of 15. The trawlers go way out into the Atlantic Ocean. They are usually gone for two weeks.

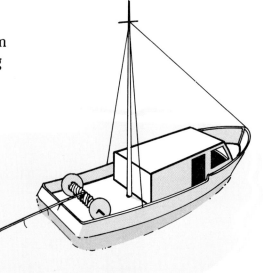

A trawler uses a net to catch fish. The enormous net is shaped like a sock. This net is dropped down to the bottom of the ocean. The trawler pulls it along. The net is open at one end but not at the other.

△ The fish swim into the net and get trapped. A trawler catches a lot more fish than a longliner. The crew begins to **process** the fish while the trawler is still at sea.

Fish from trawlers and longliners are brought to Burgeo. The most common fish is cod. About 350 people work at the fish **processing plant** in town. There, the fish are cleaned, packaged and frozen. Much of the fish gets sent to other countries. Some of the cod may become the "fish" for "fish and chips" in other parts of Canada. And, of course, the people of Burgeo eat a lot of fish, too.

A person is mending a net. What other jobs must be done on a fishing boat?

On one wall of the cabin, there was a photograph of Cammy holding up a gigantic fish. It looked almost as big as she was. Morgan looked at it so long that Cammy suggested she keep it as a souvenir.

"Oh, by the way," said Cecil, "this is where we keep the fish." He slid back a heavy, wooden cover. He explained that the cover prevents water from getting into the boat's hold. The fish were kept there after they had been caught. Morgan looked down. She couldn't believe her eyes. Instead of one or two fish, there were hundreds. Maybe even thousands. She'd never seen so many fish in all her life.

Cecil elbowed Cammy. They both laughed. Morgan looked up, confused.

"He's just a big teaser," Cammy explained to her. "They spent the whole day catching these fish."

"What will you do with all these fish?" Morgan asked.

"In a few minutes, we'll take them to the fish processing plant." Cecil explained. "The people there cut away the guts and the bones and heads. Then the fish are shipped all over the world."

How often do you eat fish? What kind of fish do you like best?

Morgan knew it was time to head back to her own home. She and Cammy climbed up onto the wharf. She was glad to feel solid ground beneath her feet. She didn't mind being a landlubber at all.

"Wait a minute," Cecil shouted. Then he climbed down into the hold. When he reappeared, he was holding a big fish. "Give this to Mrs. Parker," he said to the two girls. "Tell her it's my birthday present to her."

The fish was so big and slippery both girls had to carry it. Morgan felt a bit silly struggling to haul a fish through Burgeo. Cammy didn't seem to mind. After a short while Morgan didn't mind either. "What's so silly about carrying a fish through Burgeo?" she asked herself. "That's what people always do in a fishing town."

The cabin of the longliner has a two-way radio. When might the fisherman use it?

Back in Mrs. Parker's house, Morgan and Cammy could hear music and dancing. They approached Mrs. Parker with their fish.

"This is Uncle Cecil's gift to you for your birthday," Cammy explained.

Morgan noticed the woman with the TV camera coming in for a close-up picture. She let go of her end of the fish. It was too heavy for Cammy to hold by herself. It slid into Mrs. Parker's lap. Those watching began laughing, but Morgan didn't stop to notice. She leaped into the TV camera. She found herself back in her own quiet living room. On the TV screen in her house, she could see the people in Mrs. Parker's living room. They were all laughing now. Mrs. Parker was laughing, too.

"Just what I need," said Mrs. Parker. "A lapful of fish."

What did Morgan learn from Mrs. Parker? What could you learn from older people in your community?

What is your decision?

Television came to Burgeo in the 1960s. There is only one channel, but TV has made a big difference.

Cammy watches a lot of TV. She can see what life is like in the big cities. She learns about other people and places. She even likes watching commercials to see the new games and fashions.

Mrs. Parker doesn't like her great-great-great-grandchildren watching so much TV. She says that children don't help around the house anymore. They don't play outside as much. Mrs. Parker says that TV makes people think of leaving Burgeo. They want to move to a big city with movie theatres and department stores.

How much TV do you watch?

What do you think is good about TV?

What do you think is bad about TV?

Do you think children should have rules for watching TV?

Thinking about Burgeo

Links with Burgeo

In this book you are learning how communities are linked to one another. Each of these sentences tells one way that Burgeo links Canadians. Match each sentence with a picture in this chapter.

1. Fish caught by people from Burgeo is sent to other communities.
2. A ferry links Burgeo with other communities.
3. A road links Burgeo with Stephenville.

Working Together

Pretend you and your partner are working on a fishing boat. The sea is rough. The boat is being tossed by the waves. Plan a skit showing what you would do. Perform your skit for the class.

Comparing Communities

Add Burgeo to your Comparing Communities chart. Put information about Burgeo in its row. Compare Burgeo with another community on your chart. Can you find ways in which they are the same? Find ways in which they are different.

Community	Products	Trans-portation	Recreation	Tourist Places	Language
Your Community					
Burgeo					

This chart is used to find the distances between communities. It tells you how far you would need to travel by road from one community to another.

To find out how far it is by road from Burgeo to Stephenville, this is what you do. First, you find the names of the two communities on the chart. With your left hand follow the column that runs down from Burgeo. With your right hand follow the row that runs across from Stephenville. The column and the row meet at number 215. This means that it is 215 km from Burgeo to Stephenville.

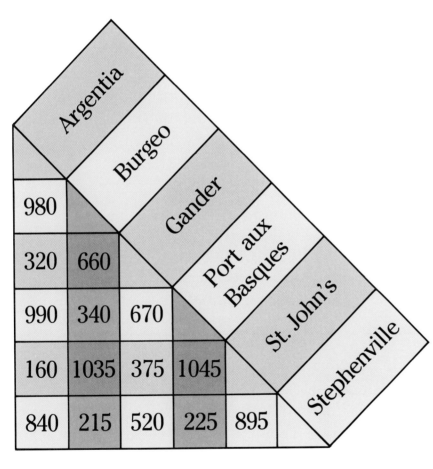

kilometres

1. How far is it from Burgeo to Port aux Basques by road? Follow the column down from Burgeo. Follow the row across from Port aux Basques.

2. Look at the map of Newfoundland on page 86. Find Burgeo and Port aux Basques. With your finger, trace the route by road between the two communities. What is a shorter way to travel from Burgeo to Port aux Basques?

3. Look at the map on page 86. Pick any two of the communities. With your finger, trace the route by road. Use this chart to find the distance between the two communities.

7

What do Cape Dorset's artists teach Canadians?

Page 101: Kenojuak Ashevak is drawing at home. Why might a person want to become an artist?

The school year was almost over. Morgan was home from school with a cold. She decided to watch the educational TV program. On the screen, a woman was drawing with coloured pencils. Morgan wanted a closer look at the bright colours. So, once again, she climbed into the TV.

The cameraperson was scowling. Morgan tried to cheer him up. "Hi! It's me again," she said. The man still did not look amused. Morgan got out of his way as quickly as possible.

She turned to watch the woman who was drawing. The woman looked up and spoke. But Morgan didn't understand a single word. Just then, a young girl who looked Morgan's age came in from the kitchen.

"Hi! I'm Pudlo," she said to Morgan. "My mother's name is Kenojuak. She speaks only ***Inuktitut***. It's the language of our people. She's wondering if you'd like to help her colour the drawings."

"Sure," Morgan said. Morgan liked drawing and colouring, in fact.

Kenojuak spoke. Again Pudlo **translated** the words. "My mother says that she's drawing pictures of spirits." Kenojuak nodded and smiled at Morgan. Morgan nodded and smiled back.

Pudlo told Morgan about her community. She lived in a village called Cape Dorset. It is a small community in the Northwest Territories. Cape Dorset is on a small island.

Kenojuak and Pudlo belonged to a group of people called the **Inuit**. The Inuit live in the **Arctic** in the far north of Canada. There are only tiny, remote villages in this region. During much of December and January, the sun only shines for a short time every day. It is always quite dark. It gets very, very cold. And yet, in the summer, the sun will shine during the night. Even in the summer there are **icebergs** in the ocean. That's the way it is in the Arctic.

Kenojuak explained that people in the rest of the world were curious about the life of the Inuit. So Kenojuak and some of her friends drew pictures. In these, they showed life in the Arctic. They also drew pictures about the old times showing how the Inuit hunted and fished. Some of Kenojuak's drawings were even about her daydreams. She was an artist.

Morgan learned that many other artists also live in Cape Dorset. Only 850 people live in the village, but people all over the world have heard of it. The pictures that Kenojuak and her friends make are famous. The sculptures made in Cape Dorset are also famous. People buy this art to decorate their homes and offices. You can see Inuit art in **museums** and **art galleries**, too.

Have you ever seen any Inuit drawings or sculptures?

This is Cape Dorset in the winter. The sun is very low in the sky, even at noon. What can you tell about the town from this picture?

102

Top: Icebergs are beautiful, but also dangerous. Why do you think they are dangerous?

Below: The picture of the children was taken in June. What can you tell about the climate in summer?

Cape Dorset

Making Inuit Prints

There are over 60 artists in Cape Dorset. Most of them work at home drawing on paper or carving **soapstone**. When an artist has finished, the art is brought to the West Baffin Eskimo Co-op. This is a group of buildings in the middle of Cape Dorset.

If the artist has drawn an interesting picture, it goes into the workshop. There, the picture is carved onto a perfectly flat stone by a stone-carver. Ink is put on the stone.

A piece of paper is laid on the stone covered with ink. One person presses the paper with a soft pad and a wooden spoon. The ink goes into the paper. This is called a stone-cut **print**. This is done over and over. Each time a print is made.

Other people in the co-op arrange a big show. The art goes on sale in one of Canada's large cities. The soapstone carvings go on sale, too. Now, all over the world, people know about the Inuit. This is because millions of people have seen the drawings of Kenojuak and her friends. The drawings have been put on stamps and in books. Movies have been made about the Inuit artists and their art.

Much of the money from the sale of the art then returns to Cape Dorset. The artists and the printmakers are paid. The money also helps the Inuit do other things in their community. In Cape Dorset, the co-op owns three trucks and delivers fuel oil. It also runs the local **weather station**. The co-op runs one of the two department stores, too. The co-op is the biggest **business** in town. It helps almost everyone.

Morgan helped Kenojuak colour in one of the drawings. As Pudlo translated, Kenojuak said, "Maybe someday your work will be in an art gallery." Morgan liked that idea a lot. She wouldn't mind being famous.

Kenojuak decided to take her drawings to the co-op. This was the building owned by all the artists. They all helped to run it. That was why it was called a co-operative. Kenojuak wanted to show the other artists her work. She invited Morgan and Pudlo along. Together they walked down the dirt road into the centre of town.

"What a strange place!" Morgan thought to herself. There wasn't a tree or a bush around. There wasn't even much grass. The ground was mostly bare rock and gravel. The houses in Cape Dorset were small and many of them looked exactly the same. Snowmobiles sat outside some of the houses.

Cape Dorset has about 200 snowmobiles, 25 trucks and only one car. What does this tell you about Cape Dorset?

Left: You can see Cape Dorset on the north side of the island. Describe the land around Cape Dorset.

Above: Why are boats important to people in Cape Dorset?

Left: Buildings must be kept off the ground. The heat from buildings might "melt" the frozen ground. What might happen then?

Cape Dorset

Helping People in a Small Community

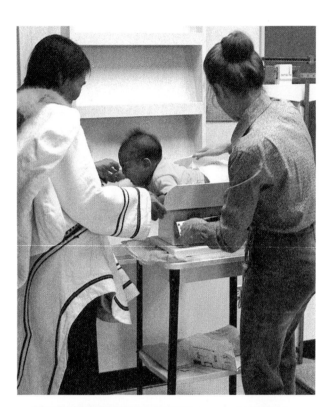

Cape Dorset is a very small community. It is too small to have a hospital. Instead, it has a nursing station. Three nurses work there and look after the community's medical needs. Every once in a while, a dentist will fly into Cape Dorset, too. But mostly, the people who are sick or injured depend on the nurses.

If someone needs to go to hospital, the nurses send for help. They will telephone to Frobisher Bay, 400 km away. A plane will be sent to Cape Dorset. The patient will be put on the plane. The plane will fly to Frobisher Bay. Frobisher Bay has the only hospital on Baffin Island.

△ Most communities in the Arctic are too small to have all the services that a big town has. Cape Dorset has a school. But if students want to finish high school, they must leave the village. The school there doesn't have the higher grades. Some students move to Frobisher Bay to go to high school. They are separated from their families. Many students get very lonely and return to Cape Dorset without finishing school.

People in small Arctic villages help one another. Often there is no road to another community. Ships and barges can reach villages in the Arctic only during the summer. There may be airplane flights to the bigger towns once or twice a week. Villages still depend on bigger towns for some services. That is the way of life in the Arctic.

What can you see that shows the traditional way of life? What shows the modern way?

Inside the co-op, Kenojuak chatted with two of her friends. They all spoke *Inuktitut*.

While Kenojuak and her friends talked, Morgan and Pudlo wandered outside. Not far away, Morgan could see a small motorboat sitting on the beach. The motorboat was being loaded by an Inuit family. They were carrying supplies to the boat. The children helped. One of the boys was carrying a rifle. Morgan asked a girl where she was going. The Inuit girl smiled. She had long, black braids tied with rubber bands.

"Now that it's almost summer," she said, "we're going to live out on the land. The sea ice has nearly melted. We do this every year. My parents say we must keep our **traditions**. We live in a tent all July and August. We learn about the old Inuit ways. My father teaches my four brothers to hunt. And my mother teaches my sister and me to sew. She also teaches me how to carve soapstone. I want to be an artist one day. Sometimes, my parents tell us stories about the old times."

To Morgan, it sounded so different. She wondered what it would be like to live in a tent all summer without electricity or TV. She wouldn't mind. Then she would know a little bit about the old way of life.

What would you like to learn about living on the land? Who could teach you?

Top: The Inuit woman is scraping sealskin with a curved knife. This is a traditional tool. What might she do with the sealskin?

Bottom: The caribou is shedding its shaggy coat. What time of year do you think it is?

Top: In May, the sky is light at night. How would the sky look in winter?

Bottom: This Inuit family lives on the land in the summer.

Morgan watched the Inuit girl get into the boat. Then she and Pudlo started back to the co-op to find the TV crew. She felt rather odd. She had travelled all over Canada. Cape Dorset was—by far—the most unusual place she'd been. It *looked* so different. But the children wore clothes like hers. They went to school and watched TV. Yet they also did things that Morgan had never done. Each summer, the whole family would live on the land. The parents would teach the children about nature and the past. It was like going to school in the summer, without home-work and quizzes.

Morgan didn't want to leave Cape Dorset. She had learned about a whole new way of life that she'd never thought of before.

Cape Dorset is an isolated village. There is no road to other places. Imagine that you live in an isolated village. What things would you like? What things wouldn't you like?

112

Morgan found Kenojuak and the TV crew. They had just started the program about the co-op business. Morgan walked quietly up beside Kenojuak and whispered, "Goodbye."

Kenojuak spoke to Morgan in *Inuktitut*. Pudlo explained, "My mother wants you to have the drawing." Morgan felt very pleased.

"Would you put your name on it?" Morgan asked. Morgan now knew that Kenojuak was famous.

Kenojuak signed the drawing. Then she held it out for Morgan to sign, too.

Morgan took the pencil and signed her name below Kenojuak's. Then Morgan scrambled into the camera.

She landed on the living room floor. Just as she got to her feet, her father came in. "What have you been doing?" he asked.

"Oh, I've been studying the Arctic," Morgan answered. She thought she'd better not show him the drawing. She suspected that her father wouldn't believe her story. So she went upstairs to draw some original Morgan McCloskey pictures. She might even autograph them if someone asked.

Kenojuak draws pictures about life in the Arctic. Other people write stories. Which tells about life better, a drawing or a story?

114

What is your decision?

Quartag is 12 years old. He lives in Cape Dorset. His family is going to leave Cape Dorset for the summer. They will hunt seals and go fishing. They will be able to get some of their food for the winter. The children will learn how to clean skins and make clothes. Quartag's parents want their children to learn how to live on the land. This is how the Inuit lived for many, many years.

Quartag doesn't want to go with them this summer. He wants to stay in Cape Dorset with his aunt. Quartag likes to see the ship unload the supplies. This only happens once a year. New games, clothes, food and heavy machines will be unloaded at Cape Dorset.

How might Quartag's parents feel if he stays in Cape Dorset for the summer?

Why would Inuit parents want their children to learn to hunt and make clothes?

Do you think it is a good idea for Inuit children to learn traditional skills?

Thinking about Cape Dorset

Links with Cape Dorset

In this book you are learning how people and communities are linked together. Each of these sentences tells one way that Cape Dorset links Canadians. Match each sentence with a picture from this chapter.

1. Inuit prints are sold in communities across Canada.
2. A barge brings supplies to Cape Dorset once a year.
3. Small planes bring people and supplies to Cape Dorset every week.

Working Together

Work in a small group to make a Cape Dorset mobile. Draw pictures on heavy paper or cardboard. One group could draw Arctic animals that live on the land. Another group could draw Arctic birds. A third group could draw Arctic animals that live in the sea. A fourth group could draw Arctic plants. Cut out your drawings. Each group can make a mobile by hanging them together.

Comparing Communities

Add Cape Dorset to your chart. Put information about Cape Dorset in its row.

Now your chart is finished. Write a sentence telling about the information on your chart.

Community	Products	Trans-portation	Recreation	Tourist Places	Language
Your Community					
Cape Dorset					

Reading a Map

This is a map of Dorset Island. The community of Cape Dorset is on the north shore of Dorset Island. The water all around Dorset Island is called Hudson Strait. The water is at **sea level**. The island is higher than the water. The island is above sea level. But the surface of the island isn't smooth. Some places are higher than others.

The colours on this map show the height above sea level for different parts of the island. Look at the green parts of the island. The key tells you that the green parts are 0—50 m above sea level.

1. Use the key to find out the height of the yellow parts of the map.
2. What colour shows land that is 100—150 m above sea level? Point to this part on the map of Dorset Island.
3. The highest parts of Dorset Island are coloured brown. Use the key to find out the height of the brown parts of the map.
4. Pretend you are in Cape Dorset. If you walked south for 1 km, would you be walking uphill or downhill?

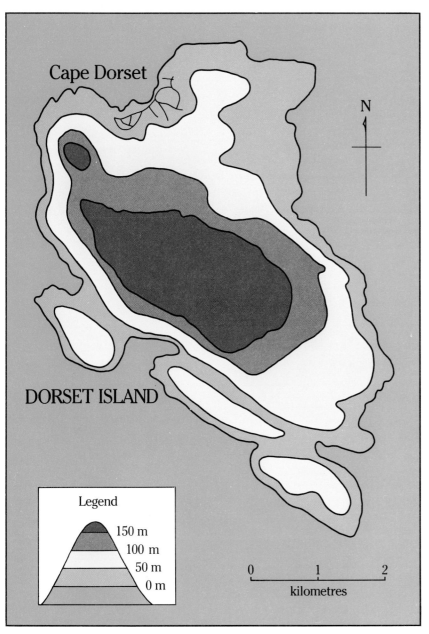

Cape Dorset

DORSET ISLAND

N

Legend
150 m
100 m
50 m
0 m

0   1   2
kilometres

8

What links Canada's communities together?

It was an exciting day for Morgan. The TV cameras had now come to Morgan's house. The TV people were making a show about her. All over Canada, Morgan had been popping in and out of cameras. No one knew how she did it. Even Morgan wasn't sure how it had happened. It was magic.

One camera followed Morgan into her room. She had all her souvenirs on the bulletin board above her desk. The red light on the camera blinked on.

The reporter asked Morgan, "Where did you get that Inuit drawing?"

Morgan smiled. The picture reminded her of the trip she'd taken to visit Kenojuak in Cape Dorset.

Far away in Cape Dorset, Kenojuak was watching TV with her friends. She saw Morgan's face on the TV screen. "There's that girl who came here last week," Kenojuak told her friends. "She helped me colour that picture."

Morgan talked about her different souvenirs. And far away, in the communities Morgan had visited, her new friends saw Morgan on TV.

In Edmonton, the reporter turned to her family. "Look at that!" she said in surprise. "That girl appeared out of nowhere last summer. We were making a show about oil in Alberta."

In Weyburn, Lars Sondquist, the farmer, looked up from his newspaper. "Hey!" There's that girl, Morgan, on TV." Mr. Sondquist's son, Gumbo, heard his father shouting. He rushed indoors. Together they watched Morgan on television.

In Sault Ste. Marie, Erik Tikkanen, the lock master, threw down his playing cards. "That's the girl who came here when the *North Wind II* almost sank."

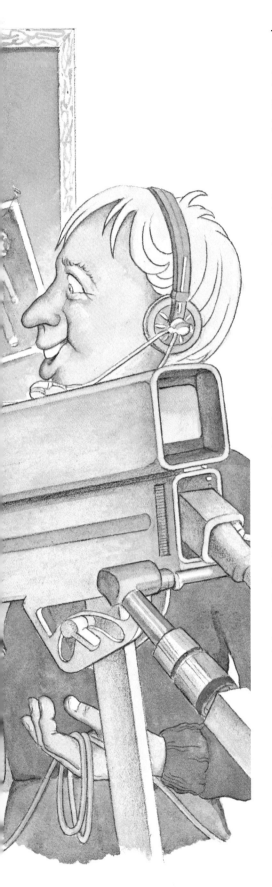

In Quebec City, the man who had dressed up as Bonhomme was watching TV. "It's a small world," he said to his wife. "Last time I saw that girl, she was right here in Quebec City enjoying Carnival."

And in Burgeo, Cecil the fisherman said to his niece Cammy, "Do you remember her?" He pointed at Morgan on the TV. Cammy remembered. It made her laugh to think of how they had dropped the fish in Cammy's great-great-great-grandmother's lap.

What communities did Morgan visit? What souvenir did she get in each place? Which is your favourite souvenir?

Morgan had learned that Canada is a big country. It is made up of many separate communities. And these communities are made up of many different people. Morgan also found out that these communities are linked together through work and play. The people in one community help those in another. That is one of the things that makes Canada a **nation**.

Morgan understood now that *all* of Canada is her country. She knew that her community is an important part of Canada. Morgan realized, too, that other Canadian communities are an important part of her.

Morgan had just begun to explore Canada. Who knows where she might travel in the future?

Glossary

This glossary tells you the meaning of some new words used in this book. Some of the words have other meanings, too. You will need a dictionary to find the other meanings.

A number is listed after each of the meanings. This number tells you the page where the new word is first used. The word is in heavy print on that page. You can read more about the word there. The pictures will tell you more, too.

Some of the new words are hard to say. To help you, they are respelled as they sound.

a =	cat	i =	it	u =	up
ā =	say	ī =	ride	ù =	look
e =	red	o =	dog	ü =	school
ē =	he	ō =	go	ə =	pocket

′ is an accent mark. It points to the part of the word that you say most strongly.

jump′ ing
good bye′

ancestor (an′ ses tr): a family member who lived long ago. Your great-grandparents and your great-great-grandparents are some of your ancestors. (p. 57)

Arctic (Ark′ tik): the land and sea around the north pole. In Canada, part of the Yukon Territory and the Northwest Territories is in the Arctic. (p. 100)

art gallery: a building where people can see and learn about works of art. There are pictures, carvings and other beautiful things in an art gallery. (p. 102)

au revoir (ō′ rə vwor): French words that mean goodbye. (p. 76)

blizzard (bliz′ rd): a very bad storm with snow and high winds. (p. 40)

business (biz′ nəs): a place where people go to buy or sell things. Grocery stores and gas stations are businesses. (p. 105)

canal (kə nal′): a waterway made by people. Most canals are built for ships to travel along. (p. 46)

capital: a city where the government meets to make plans and laws. Each province in Canada has a capital city. Canada has a capital city for the whole country, too. (p. 6)

citizen: a person who lives in a community. (p. 21)

combine (kom′ bīn): a farm machine that can cut down grain and then separate grain seeds from straw. A combine is often used just for separating the grain seeds. (p. 33)

conveyor (kən vā′ yr): a long moving belt that carries things from one place to another. A conveyor carries grain up to the storage bins in a grain elevator. (p. 38)

co-operative (kō op′ r a tiv): a business that is owned by the people who use it or by the workers. The short form of co-operative is co-op. (p. 36)

country: a land where the people have the same main government. Canada is a country and so is the United States. (p. 6)

cultural: having to do with culture. Canadians come from many cultural backgrounds. (p. 61)

culture: the beliefs and special ways of living that a group of people have. Some things that might be part of a person's culture are food, clothing, language, religion, art, songs, stories and dances. (p. 61)

elect: to choose people to run the government. The people in a community vote for the person they think is best. The person with the most votes is elected. (p. 72)

election (ē lek′ shun): the time when everyone votes for people to run the government. (p. 74)

factory: a large building where things like shoes, cars and cloth are made. (p. 18)

fertile: able to produce a lot of something. Plants grow well in fertile soil. (p. 32)

foreign (fōr′ ən): from another country. (p. 56)

fuel: something that is burned to make heat or power. The fuel that most car engines burn is gasoline. (p. 12)

government: the people elected to make rules for a community, province or country. The government provides many services for the people. (p. 21)

grain: this word has two meanings in this book:

    1. a plant with hard seeds, like wheat, rye, oats, barley and corn. (p. 32)

    2. the seeds of grain plants. Grain is ground into flour to make bread, cakes, cookies and noodles. (p. 33)

grain elevator: a tall building where wheat, barley and other grains are stored. Farmers bring their grain to a grain elevator. (p. 36)

grain terminal: a tall building used for storing grain in a port. A large grain terminal can hold more wheat than 50 grain elevators. (p. 39)

harvest: to pick or cut down ripe food from fields or gardens. Wheat is harvested in the fall. (p. 30)

hopper car: a railway car for carrying grain. A hopper car is loaded from the top, and unloaded from the bottom. (p. 38)

hyvästi (hi vas′ tē): a Finnish word that means goodbye. (p. 60)

iceberg: a huge piece of ice floating in the sea. Most of an iceberg is under the water. (p. 100)

Inuit (I′ nyü it): native people who live in the far north. Inuit means "the people." (p. 100)

Inuktitut (I′ nyük ti tyüt): the language that the Inuit speak. It is written with a different alphabet. (p. 100)

island (ī′ land): a piece of land that has water on all sides. Some islands are very large while others are tiny. (p. 88)

lanttu laatikko (lan′ tü lo′ ti kō): a Finnish casserole or stew made with turnips. (p. 56)

law: a rule that people must live by. Laws are made by governments. (p. 72)

Le Carnaval de Québec (Lə Kar′ na′ val′ də Kā bek′): the French name for a winter festival held each year in Quebec City. (p. 64)

lock: a waterway to raise and lower ships. (p. 48)

longliner: a fishing boat that drags very long fishing lines behind it. (p. 90)

loppet (lo′ pet): a word used in Finland that means a race for fun. (p. 58)

mojakka (moi′ ə ku): a Finnish stew or thick soup made with fish. (p. 57)

mother tongue: the first language a person learns to speak. The mother tongue is the language that people usually use at home. (p. 79)

multi-cultural (mul′ tē kul′ chr əl): having many different cultures. Canada is a multi-cultural country. (p. 61)

museum (myü zē′ um): a building where people can see interesting things. At a museum, people learn how others lived long ago. (p. 102)

nation (nā′ shun): a land or country with its own government. Canada is a nation. (p. 121)

ocean (ō′ shun): a large body of salt water. The Atlantic Ocean is on the east side of Canada, the Pacific Ocean is on the west side, and the Arctic Ocean is on the north side. (p. 88)

oil: a thick, greasy liquid that is used to make gasoline, plastic and many other things. (p. 10)

oil field: a place under the ground or sea where oil has been found. (p. 12)

oil well: a hole drilled in the ground in order to get oil. (p. 10)

outport: a small town or village on the coast of Newfoundland. Most outports are far away from other towns. (p. 86)

piirakka (pēr′ ə kə): a Finnish bun or pastry with a filling. There are meat *piirakkas*, vegetable *piirakkas* and dessert *piirakkas*. (p. 57)

Place Royale (Plas Roi al′): the French name for a very old part of Quebec City. (p. 70)

port: a town or city that has a place where ships can dock. In a port, ships can load and unload cargo. (p. 39)

prairies: a flat land that is found in southern Manitoba, Saskatchewan and Alberta. Grasses and grains grow well on the prairies. (p. 32)

premier (prēm′ yr): the leader of the government of a province. (p. 72)

print: a copy of a picture or a design. (p. 105)

process (prō′ ses): to make something ready to use. (p. 93)

processing plant: a factory where fish are made ready to sell. The fish are frozen or canned or sold fresh. (p. 93)

province: one of the main parts that make up a country. Canada has ten provinces. British Columbia is one province, Ontario is another. (p. 6)

pulla (pü′ lə): a Finnish coffee bread that is flavoured with a spice called cardamom. (p. 57)

rapids: a place in a river where the water runs very quickly. Often there are big rocks in the rapids and boats cannot travel over them. (p. 50)

refinery: a building where things like oil, sugar or metals are made ready to sell. In an oil refinery, oil from the ground is cleaned and made into gasoline, grease and other things. (p. 14)

rue Ste-Thérèse (rü′ Sənt Tā rez′): French words meaning Saint Theresa Street. (p. 66)

sea level: where the top of the sea is. The edge of a beach is at sea level. (p. 117)

shore: the place where the land meets a sea or a lake. (p. 88)

signal: a way of sending someone a message. There are hand signals, flag signals and colour signals. (p. 48)

soapstone: a soft stone that is used for carving. Soapstone is usually grey or green with streaks of darker colour through it. (p. 104)

territory: a special part of Canada. Canada's two territories are the Yukon Territory and the Northwest Territories. The territories are large and have a small number of people. (p. 8)

tourist: a person visiting a place for pleasure. (p. 71)

tractor: a farm machine that is used to pull a plow and other things. (p. 12)

tradition (trə di′ shun): something that people have done in the same way for a very long time. For some families, it is a tradition to eat turkey at Thanksgiving. (p. 110)

translate: to change speech or writing from one language to another. (p. 100)

trawler: a large fishing boat that pulls a net behind it to catch fish. (p. 92)

volunteer: a person who does some work but does not get paid for it. (p. 20)

weather station: a place where people study the weather and make notes about it. The information from weather stations is used to forecast the weather. (p. 105)

wharf (wōrf): a platform where ships can tie up. (p. 88)

Explorations A Canadian Social Studies Program for Elementary Schools

Exploring Families

Families Are People
Families Have Needs
Families Share
Families Are Special
Families Change
Families Have Feelings

Exploring Communities

Exploring Your School and Neighbourhood
Exploring a Space Community
Exploring Mount Currie
Exploring Elkford
Exploring Prince George
Exploring Naramata

Exploring Canada

Exploring British Columbia's Past
Exploring Our Country
Turn On To Canada

Exploring Canada's Past

The Haida and the Inuit: People of the Seasons
The Explorers: Charting the Canadian Wilderness

Exploring Canada's Past, Present and Future

Exploring Canada: Learning from the Past, Looking to the Future

Exploring the World

Exploring Our World: Other People, Other Lands

Acknowledgements

Photographs
Algoma Kinniwabi Travel Association:
p. 59, top.
Scott Alpen/Image Finders: p. 12, top; p. 4,
left; p. 12, bottom.
Bob Anderson/Masterfile: pp. 30-31, bottom.
Craig Aurness/Image Finders: p. 35, bottom;
p. 38, top.
Steve Birrel/West Baffin Eskimo Co-
operative Ltd.: p. 109, bottom.
R.H. Blanchet/Image Finders: p. 33, bottom
right.
Ray Chen/Masterfile: p. 75, bottom.
Nicholas Coroluick/Charnell Studio: p. 37,
right.
Ted Czolowski/Image Finders: p. 67, top;
p. 69, bottom.
Lauren Dale: p. 11; pp. 18-19; pp. 20-21,
bottom; p. 22; pp. 22-23, bottom; p. 25, top;
p. 25, bottom.
John de Visser/Masterfile: p. 39, bottom;
p. 104, top; p. 104, bottom left; p. 105, top
left; pp. 106-107, bottom centre.
Dykstra Photos/Image Finders: p. 79,
bottom left.
Dan Fivehouse/Image Finders: p. 79, bottom
right.
Ed Gifford/Photo/Graphics: p. 29; p. 35, top;
p. 38, top.
Glenbow Museum: p. 13; p. 41, top.
Ted Grant/Masterfile: p. 93, top right.
Bob Herger/Photo/Graphics: p. 33, top.
Image Finders: p. 17.

Al Koch/Image Finders: p. 40, top.
J.A. Kraulis/Masterfile: p. 16.
J.A. Kraulis/Photo/Graphics: p. 5, left;
pp. 68-69, centre.
Malak/Miller Services: pp. 70-71, top.
James Manning/West Baffin Eskimo Co-
operative Ltd.: p. 5, right; p. 101; p. 103,
middle; pp. 104-105, bottom; p. 107, right;
p. 108, top left; p. 108, bottom; p. 110, top;
p. 111, bottom; pp. 112-113, top;
pp. 112-113, bottom.
Garry Marchant: p. 65; p. 71, bottom; p. 76;
p. 77.
Frank Mayrs: p. 103, top; pp. 106-107, top;
p. 109, top; p. 111, top; p. 115, top.
National Film Board: p. 40, bottom.
Michael Neil: pp. 102-103, bottom.
NFB/Photothèque: p. 67, bottom.
Ontario Government: p. 51; p. 55, top right;
p. 55, bottom; p. 56; p. 59, bottom.
Ken Patterson/Image Finders: pp. 32-33,
bottom centre.
Pentact Group/Image Finders: p. 69, top.
Les Photographes Kedl Ltée.: p. 70, bottom;
p. 73.
Public Archives of Canada: *Shooting the
Rapids* by F.A. Hopkins, p. 50, top (C-2774);
Samuel de Champlain (in an Indian Canoe)
by P.H. DeRinzy, p. 70, top left (C-13320).
Quebec Government: p. 74, top; p. 74,
bottom.
Toby Rankin/Masterfile: p. 14, bottom right.
Saskatchewan Government: p. 32, bottom

left; p. 41, bottom.
Sault Ste. Marie and District Chamber of
Commerce: p. 4, right; p. 47; p. 52; p. 53, top.
Robert S. Semeniuk: p. 110, bottom; p. 115,
bottom.
Ken Straiton/Image Finders: p. 39, top.
Sundancer/Miller Services: pp. 92-93, top
centre.
Transport Canada: pp. 54-55, top centre.
Alvis Upitis/Image Bank: p. 4, centre; p. 31,
top.
Jürgen Vogt/Photo/Graphics: p. 5, centre;
p. 53, bottom; p. 57; p. 83; pp. 84-85, centre;
p. 85, right; p. 87, top; p. 87, bottom; p. 88,
left; pp. 88-89, bottom; p. 89, bottom right;
p. 91; p. 92, top left; pp. 92-93, bottom; p. 94;
p. 95; p. 97, top; p. 97, bottom.
Alex Waterhouse-Hayward: p. 20, bottom
left; pp. 20-21, top centre; p. 21, right;
p. 105, top right.
Roland Weber/Masterfile: pp. 74-75, top.
Daniel Wood: pp. 14-15, top; pp. 36-37,
centre; p. 49, top; p. 49, bottom; p. 64.
Cover Photographs
Bob Herger/Photo/Graphics: back cover.
Jürgen Vogt/Photo/Graphics: front cover.
Illustrations
Renée Mansfield: all illustrations, except for
the following.
Barbara Hodgson: p. 14, left; p. 50, bottom
left; p. 51, top; p. 92, bottom left.
Maps and Graphs
Karen Ewing